HEAVEN'S STAGE ON 5TH AND MAIN

Dancing Life's Greatest Jig

MJ GAYLOR

WESTBOW
PRESS®
A DIVISION OF THOMAS NELSON
& ZONDERVAN

WestBow Press books may be ordered through booksellers or by contacting:

WestBow Press
A Division of Thomas Nelson & Zondervan
1663 Liberty Drive
Bloomington, IN 47403
www.westbowpress.com
844-714-3454

ISBN: 979-8-3850-4244-9 (sc)
ISBN: 979-8-3850-4243-2 (e)

Library of Congress Control Number: 2025901542

Print information available on the last page.

WestBow Press rev. date: 01/29/2025

We know what we are but know
not what we may be.

William Shakespeare

Contents

I wish to thank Karen Gaylor, Susan
Jordan, Lillian Tuten, and Caleb Bryan
for their work in the editing process.
Their efforts are deeply appreciated.
A special thanks to Amanda Winsor
for her work with the photographs
included on the cover and interior.

⟨⟨⟨⟩⟩⟩

To our granddaughter, Lorelai. First in
pecking order, and always first in our
hearts. Your love of stage inspires us and
your passion for life keeps us always on
the front row. Kiki and I love you dearly.
You are truly dancing life's greatest jig.

Prologue

We are presently living in the prologue of a story we call time. It is the opening act of a play that has no end. When the first Act is finished, we will enter either a glorious ongoing story in heaven or a disastrous ruin in hell. There are no gray shadowlands; no exists into the dark alleyway of oblivion. We will then discover that the great divide we have long suspected is true and the two destinations are eternal in nature. For you see, the human spirit, having been given by God, is as immortal as God himself.

Thankfully, God's stage comes with an opportunity and a choice. The part we play in his story is yet to be determined; but know this, when the curtain drops on our lives, our part in the production cannot be rewritten. Decisions this side of the veil are important beyond calculation. Our choice to embrace the Playwright and become a part of his story begins with a decision to join heaven's stage troupe and journey into the greatest story ever told.

It has always been the cry of the human heart to find a purpose greater than itself. It is the deepest longing of the soul to be caught up in a cause so glorious that it transcends life itself. It is my hope that you will see, perhaps for the very first time, that the hand of the Playwright has been present from life's first cry to your final breath. He has always been there, and his desire is for you to understand and believe his message concerning his Son. Your life presents an opportunity to fulfill his great design. Lift up your eyes and open your heart. Behold, the great stage and story of the Playwright awaits you.

CHAPTER 1

The curtain rises

William Shakespeare was a literary genius. His ability to develop characters and twist plots is legendary. In his pastoral comedy, *As You Like It*, the Bard of Avon places on the lips of the melancholy Jacques this famous and perceptive monologue concerning life, "All the world is a stage, and all the men and women merely players; they have their exits and their entrances, and one man in his time plays many parts, his acts being changes." (2.7.146) Alas, such is life on this spinning globe, or should I say, grand earthly stage.

In the following pages, it is my desire to elevate Shakespeare's definitive assessment of life's expansive drama to a higher plain. The stage on which we are living out our lives is greater than we can imagine and more majestic than we can appreciate. Furthermore, the fine wooden boards on which we dance, sing, and deliver our lines are nothing less than heaven's platform. All of heaven, as well as earth, *is* a stage, and there is not an empty seat in this celestial auditorium.

Accordingly, our value as human beings is not determined by this world but by this very simple truth: we have all been cast in a tale larger than ourselves. We all play a part that only we can fill. To know this truth is to begin to hear the heart of the Director of heaven. To live this truth is to dance life's greatest jig. Let us travel back to our opening scene.

When the earthly curtain rose in our first moments, a much-anticipated tale of adventure began. To begin with, the doctor and nurses attending our mother were not alone in the room. Angels, filled with excitement, crowded in to witness the event. These supernatural beings directed the stage lights as skilled musicians tuned their instruments in the orchestra pit. The beat of a kettle drum grew louder until our first cry caused the stringed instruments to leap into action. The woodwinds followed, dancing along with the cries of our protest from being ripped from the warmth of our mother's womb. A golden harp played softly as the nurse laid us gently on our mother's chest. A new member had joined the troupe of God's great redemptive story.

Medical professionals, oblivious to the presence of these heavenly beings, performed their duties as the great drama of a life began. The angels held their breath in anticipation of which heavenly spirit would be assigned to our care. Jockeying for position, they all had their hands thrust in the air. Perhaps, I have allowed my imagination to run wild, but regardless, we know that God was in the room, and he was excited about our arrival.

Likewise, it matters not the circumstances surrounding our arrival. With each new baby comes a life full of potential, and with every child there is a tale to be told. Rich or poor, wanted or unwanted, we have all been fashioned for a very specific purpose. Unbeknown to us, we have all been in the spotlight of the Playwright's glorious production from the very beginning. We were created for the glory of God, and long before our first breath, the Lord knew us intimately.

David, the sweet Psalmist of Israel, picked up his quill and wrote down one of the most beautiful revelations concerning the Lord's knowledge of those he created. He writes, "For you formed my inward parts; you knitted me together in my mother's womb. My frame was not hidden from you, when I was being made in secret, intricately woven in the depths of the earth. Your eyes saw my unformed substance; in your book were written, every one of them, the days that were formed for me, when as yet there was none of them."[1] The thought was overwhelming to David. Every detail of his life was fully known by his Creator before his first breath.

Furthermore, he mused, "O Lord, you have searched me and known me! You know when I sit down and when I rise up; you discern my thoughts from afar. You search out my path and my lying down and are acquainted with all my ways. Even before a word is on my tongue, behold, O Lord, you know it all together."[2]

David could not make a move or think a thought without the Director's knowledge. Wherever he journeyed, the Lord was fully present, even in his lowest moments and especially in his worst times. "If I ascend up into heaven, thou art there: if I make my bed in hell, behold, thou art there."[3] David worked himself into a crescendo of praise, declaring with astonishment, that he, a lonely shepherd boy, was "fearfully and wonderfully made."[4]

As thrilled as our parents were to welcome us into their home, heaven's excitement was greater. Angels sat on the edge of their seats, listening for our first words and watching our first steps. Furthermore, our appearance on life's stage was no surprise to the Director. He did not have to scramble to find us a part. God passed no one aside to make room for us. He had a perfect role designed according to our natural gifts.

It is important to note that our fanbase extends beyond our limited lookout, and our part in God's production is applauded by an audience of epic proportions. Heaven's theater is full of angelic beings just waiting to see how our story plays out. At our birth the angels cried, "It's showtime." Our daily performance is viewed and discussed around water fountains in the courts of heaven.

The Bible itself is filled with the topic of angels and their interest in mankind. The Apostle Peter wrote this… "It was revealed to them, that they were serving not themselves but you, in the things that have now been announced to you through those who preached the good news to you by the Holy Spirit sent from Heaven, *things into which angels long to look.*" (emphasis mine)[5] The Greek word for *long* carries with it the idea of a deep desire to view something amazing. Heavenly beings love the writings of the great Playwright as he pens his redemptive story through mankind. These angelic hosts are filled with curiosity as they keep a close eye on the recipients of salvation, and for that matter, the rest of humanity. Beyond Peter's quill, Jesus himself gave us insight into heaven's audience.

Consider the words of the Master concerning the children who flocked to him, "See that you do not despise one of these little ones. For I tell you that in Heaven their angels always see the face of my Father who is in Heaven."[6] The reference to *their* angels suggests that we each have a guardian angel assigned to us.

My sister, Phyllis, recently shared this memory, "I was very little but big enough to sleep in a single bed. We lived in an apartment on W. Main Street at the time. Mine was a small, narrow room and at the end of my bed stood a tall free-standing closet. One night when it was dark I looked up and saw an angel sitting on top of that cabinet. I remember it was a very white light. I knew by its shape that it was an angel. I didn't say a word; I just looked and then it was gone."

It is a wonderful thought that our own personal guardian angel is always present, always ministering to us. Directing the traffic of our busy lives, they must shake their heads at times. Close calls with death are not simply good luck, they are examples of the Playwright's providential protection, quite possibly through angels.

Baby Moses floated down the Nile River past hungry crocodiles and into the safety of Pharaoh's daughter. He was not alone in those muddy, reed-filled waters as angels pushed his basket along. The prostitute Rahab survived the fall of Jericho when all her neighbors were crushed in the rubble. The support beams in the wall surrounding her apartment held fast, or perhaps, they were being held up. For Gideon, God assembled an army of only 300 to deliver Israel from the hordes of Midianites. They blew their trumpets and lit up the countryside with candles from their broken pitchers. They shouted, "The Sword of the Lord and of Gideon." The Midianites, who appeared as a swarm of grasshoppers, began killing one another. The presence and influence of angels have not diminished with the passage of time. Angels are still active today, albeit, hidden from our view.

Unfortunately, the mystery of angelic involvement in our lives appears to us as something distant and mysterious. We know angels are real, but they feel shadowy and far away. In our pragmatic, work-a-day world, we have lost a sense of wonder at the possibility of these unseen beings protecting and surrounding us. We all tend to lose the marvel of a child in our march through life. When viewing a sunset or a full moon, our minds can easily become distracted with life's many cares. In those moments, we should be musing rather than being weighed down by life's worries.

Melanie Warner and Amber Torres, in their book, *Angels Among Us*, include the story of Laura Annette Duncan, who, in 1974, lived in North Tucson, Arizona. Laura was working one night at a gas station when she was approached by a man who was both handsome and charming. Reluctantly, she agreed to meet him after her shift. As she tells the story, "Looking out the window at closing, I thought it was a little strange that he had parked out by the road instead of in front of the store, but I was still focused on closing out my shift. As I was counting money I heard a woman's voice yell loudly and urgently, "Don't go out!!!" It was like someone was screaming, only inside my head. But it was as clear as if someone was standing next to me."[7] She left out the back door and rode her bike home. It was not until years later when she discovered that the man who was waiting for her was none other than Ted Bundy, the serial killer. There is little doubt that angels were warning her of the impending danger.

Angelic beings also desire to *investigate* the affairs of men regarding the unfolding story of redemption. Consider the following amazing truth concerning angels. With all the majesty of creation before their eyes, the one captivating topic that fascinates their keen intellect is the work of God in the lives of men. During the intermission, they refuse to go get popcorn or a drink in the event they might miss an important twist in the plot. They just simply can't get enough of the story. They sit on the edge of their seats, looking up at the Playwright, waiting for the next shoe to drop. With inquisitive looks on their faces, they watch with bated breath as the story unfolds.

In the movie, *It's a Wonderful Life*, George Bailey was at the end of his rope. Old man Potter had painted him into a corner, and he was considering a nighttime dip in an icy river. An angel named Clarence was sent down from heaven to reveal to George that his life was really quite wonderful. When George's dreams were repeatedly crushed by circumstances, he despaired. His guardian angel, Clarence, showed him that despite every downturn, God had a purpose. George Bailey discovered that the love of family and friends was far more valuable than his dreams. Clarence finally got his wings.

The three angels who dropped by Abraham's tent on the plains of Mamre were there for more than just a social call. The Angel of the Lord, who was none other than the pre-incarnate Christ, allowed the father of the Jewish nation to negotiate terms concerning the destruction of Sodom. When the judgment of Sodom and Gomorrah fell, Lot was safely in the mountains.

An angel greeted the prophet Daniel, addressing the seer as one who was *beloved*.[8] He then proceeded to instruct the man of God regarding what would befall the children of Israel in the last days. God could have left a note on a bush or given Daniel a dream, but instead he used an angel. The prophecies that the herald gave Daniel are being fulfilled even in our day. The messages that angels deliver, though, are not always positive. At times, they confront wayward preachers, rebuking them for their selfish spirit.

An angel with a flaming sword challenged the greedy prophet Balaam as he was on his way to curse the children of Israel.[9] The heavenly audience held their breath as the angel's sword was raised to take Balaam's life. His donkey spoke up and prevented bloodshed that day. It's possible that Balaam wasn't the only one surprised when the donkey spoke. The angels might have been caught off guard with that last minute plot twist, rocking heaven's courts with laughter. The use of a chatty mule was a stroke of brilliance by the Director.

It was an angel whom God sent to remind the Roman authorities that their power only went so far. By springing Peter from the slammer, they revealed God's script of deliverance.[10] The angel who told him to gather his stuff and exit stage left had no problem with prison doors. The usually noisy prison doors had been greased by a heavenly lubricant. When angels are involved, prisoners do not have to crawl through a sewage pipe to freedom.

Two angels sat by the empty sepulcher as three women came to anoint the body of Jesus. "Why do you seek the living among the dead," they asked. The Director could have left a sticky note, but he choose to deliver the good news through angelic beings. These women were rewarded for their devotion to Christ.

These examples of angels, mixing it up with men and women, are not exclusive to the biblical narrative. God has not suddenly changed in his dealings with mankind. Angels move and walk among us each day. Stories pile up quickly of moments we cannot explain concerning events we cannot deny. The writer of Hebrews warns, "Do not neglect to show hospitality to strangers, for thereby some have entertained angels unawares."[11]

My brother Lee was a young boy with an adventurous spirit. One late winter day he wandered off toward the stream that ran behind our house. The spring thaw had taken hold and the creek was overflowing. As Lee approached the dangerous current, dressed in his winter suit, something told my mother to check on him. She arrived just in time to rescue him from certain death. Why was our mother suddenly concerned for her son's safety and whereabouts? Could it have been Lee's guardian angel who tapped her on the shoulder? We have all experienced moments when a voice warned us, or circumstances beyond our control prevented us from being in a place that would have caused us death or harm.

There is a world among us that we do not see but is nonetheless real. There is a still small voice within us that speaks louder than the brassy tones of life if we would but listen. A. W. Tozer writes, "Every one of us has had experiences which we have not been able to explain: a sudden sense of loneliness, or a feeling of wonder or awe in the face of universal vastness. Or we have had a fleeting visitation of light like an illumination from some other sun, giving us, in a quick flash, an assurance that we are from another world, that our origins are divine." He continues, "The facts are that God is not silent, has never been silent. It is the nature of God to speak. The second Person of the Holy Trinity is called the Word."[12]

The presence of the Lord and his protective angels encourages us to boldly march into the fray and face the dangers inherit in each new day. A young Winston Churchill, having encountered the enemy in India, felt a rush of exhilaration as he boldly rode his grey pony through the fray. Having come within forty yards of the enemy Churchill saw the whites of their eyes and it spurred him onto greatness in battle. Knowing that we have a heavenly audience encourages us in the race set before us. "Therefore, since we are surrounded by so great a cloud of witnesses, let us also lay aside every weight, and sin which clings so closely, and let us run with endurance the race that is set before us."[13]

God is involved in every life in every moment we are alive. Our lives matter beyond our wildest dreams and aspirations simply because we live and draw breath. As Paul told the people of Athens, "And he made from one man every nation of mankind to live on all the face of the earth, having determined allotted periods and the boundaries of their dwelling place, that they should seek God and perhaps feel their way toward him and find him. Yet, he is actually not far from each one of us, for "'In him we live and move and have our being'; as even some of your own poets have said "'For we are indeed his offspring.'"[14] When someone takes time to speak to us, and listen, it reveals that they value us.

Dr. Seuss, in his book, *Horton Hears A Who!*, chronicles the story of an elephant named Horton who hears a tiny yelp coming from a speck of dust. Convinced that this noise is a cry for help, he places the speck on top of a pink clover. On this speck, he discovers Whoville, inhabited by the Who people led by Mayor Ned McDodd. Ned, along with his wife Sally, enjoy a family of 96 daughters, all with a name beginning with H. Their one son, JoJo is a quiet, young man, and with that many sisters, you can understand why. However, the real reason JoJo says little is because he does not want to disappoint his father. His father desires him to one day become mayor. Unfortunately, JoJo's real passion is music. In the end, Whoville is saved from destruction by the blast of JoJo's "symphonophone." Thankfully, it produces a sound that all could hear, thus proving their existence.

On this speck of dust, which is our earth, our heavenly Father hears our cry and understands the desires of our hearts. Unlike JoJo's father, he directs us down the path that we have been fashioned to travel. The Playwright has written his script on our hearts, if we will but listen. We must follow the passion placed within us by the Director. There is no reason to be quiet.

God is fully present in our lives, and he is not silent. In fact, our name was on the marquee, and our show was sold out long before we arrived at the theater. Tickets flew out of the box office when it was announced that we would be in the program. Heavenly newspapers ran front page articles in our honor. The Writer of our life's story has certain glorious ends in mind. Life's finales become perfectly merged into God's grander story. He has a very important part for us, and we have been fashioned perfectly for the role we are to play.

This truth is life transforming. He has placed every dip and dimple to cast us and regardless of present appearances, we blend beautifully with our fellow actors and actresses. We are not lonely sailors, traveling across an endless ocean, destined to be shipwrecked on a deserted island. The Director did not cast us to become castaways on *Gilligan's Island*. He has no desire for us to wander aimlessly about on a desolate island, awaiting a rescue that never comes. Life has meaning beyond collecting coconuts and being hit with the Skipper's soft cap when we muddle up a line or miss our cue. The stage is grand, and our role is thrilling beyond belief. He blends millions of amazing subplots into the central tale of redemptive history, and he desires you to a part of it. The cast is huge, and yet, your individual role is vital. The Director of heaven deeply values all his actors and actresses because he created them, and he never makes a mistake. "For the gifts and calling of God are without repentance."[15] He never regrets the gifts that he gives men and the callings he graciously extends.

Our value as cast members is not determined by our bank account or notoriety. Moreover, our significance is not determined by the part the Director has chosen for us, but in the fact he has simply included us in his story. Our station in society is irrelevant to the Director. He uses the mighty and the small with an impartiality that levels the playing field. Even the timid soul finds a special place in his story. The flowers that blooms under the mighty oak are still displaying the glory of God in their own unique way.

Our talent level is also equal to our part, and although we may increase its outflow, we can never out-stretch its potential. There are no auditions required to join the cast and no dues to be paid to the actors' guild. Most importantly, the opinions and judgments of the other actors on stage matter little in comparison to the invitation of the Lord. He always knows what he is doing despite our misgivings. Heaven's theater is strange indeed.

Every human being has a part because the casting call goes out to all people. A cattle call of chorus girls, hoping to be chosen and experience a curtain call of fame, is not in the mind of the Director. All receive the same billing. He does not pick who will populate heaven's stage and who will be cast aside for destruction. "For God so loved the *world...*" All will not respond; however, every human being is included as a potential member in the troupe.

There are also no flat characters. Every thespian displays the fullness and character God has designed. We judge the lesser or greater role by our number of lines or our opportunities to be in the limelight. However, a whisper in the darkness or a subtle glance at just the right time, is as significant to the Director as the most verbose soliloquy. More simply put, the wallflower shines as brightly as the heroic protagonist on heaven's stage. Every character is a round, full expression of the glory of God.

Years ago, Dr. Paul Brand and Philip Yancey co-authored a book titled, *Fearfully and Wonderfully Made.* Filled with amazing facts about the human body, and skillfully written to apply those discoveries to the spiritual body of Christ, the book stands as a classic that should be read by everyone. In his chapter regarding worth, Brand writes this concerning the function of a single cell..., "One who studies the vast quantity of cells, and their startling diversity can come away with a sense that each cell is easily expendable and of little consequence. But the same body that impresses us with specialization and diversity also affirms that each of its many members are valuable and often essential for survival."[16]

The Apostle Paul agrees as he uses the biblical imagery of the body regarding the church. "For just as the body is one and has many members, and all the members of the body, though many, are one body, so it is with Christ."[17] Every member of the cast brings a unique contribution to the production. The little toe carries the scene with as much force as the watery eyes. The chemistry of God's redemptive story uses each actor or actress in ways only he can devise.

Dr. Brand continues..., "Our culture is shot through with rating systems, beginning with the first grades of school when children receive marks defining relative performance. That, combined with factors such as physical appearance, popularity, and athletic prowess, may well determine how valuable people perceive themselves to be."[18]

Perhaps, you were the shortest girl in class who never got to clean the chalkboard. The nerds were always passed over when it came time to choose sides in softball. Muscle-bound athletes are rarely invited to join the debate team. These ruthless processes were brought to bear by mitigating circumstances beyond the child's control. We do not choose our athletic prowess neither our physical features. Our mental abilities are given specifically for the task at hand. However, those moments when we feel woefully inadequate can cripple us. They weld self-conceptions of worth that have nothing to do with the reality of God's story in our lives.

Personal value must be grounded in an understanding of your place in the story God has written. Understanding your worth in God's production is a pivotal moment in your life. The curtain has risen on your life. The spotlight has been turned on, lighting your path. The Playwright has included you in his story. Embrace his invitation. Will you walk in the spotlight for which you were created? The angels are watching, and they are the ultimate stagehands.

CHAPTER 2

Heaven's theater

Welcome to heaven's theater. More splendid than we can imagine, it surrounds us and calls us to its stage. Its location is every home and every heart that will open its door to its wonder. It exists to tell the story of redemption and celebrates the priceless union of Creator and creature. Heaven's theater is a place of constant activity and unending production. It's cast members come from all the tribes of the earth, and that is both its strength and beauty. Admission to this magnificent edifice has been paid for in advance. Tickets are waiting at the box office for all those who will simply come. The auditorium is already filled by the heavenly host, but the stage has plenty of room. Heaven's theater awaits the stampede of all humanity to enter its grand production. Its doors have been swung open wide, and a bullrush of eager participants should be the results.

Unfortunately, an honest appraisal paints a different picture. The masses today are standing outside in the cold and staring through the smudged windowpanes of their self-willed ignorance concerning heaven's stage. Humanity is not trumpeting the production. Life swirls around them, and they are missing the big show. Caught in a tornado of busyness, they never find the calm in the storm. The disconnect between their daily grind and the truth of God's higher calling is as wide as a Montana sky and as hidden as the Holy Grail. There seems to be a disconnect between heaven and earth which can only be described has a great chasm. Something horrible must have caused this great divide.

Achilles was a mythical Greek warrior who fought in the Trojan War. He was the son of the mortal Peleus and the sea nymph Thetis. The story, written by Homer, was an epic tale of great potential ending in a sad tragedy. Achilles served in the army of Agamemnon and proved to be a fighter of great skill and bravery. Incredibly handsome, his fame grew with every victory over the enemy until a fatal wound ended his life. In a non-Homeric account, his mother dipped Achilles in the River Styx as a baby making him invincible, but she failed to include his ankle in the baptism. This failure to plunge him completely led to his eventual downfall. In the midst of battle his heel was struck with an arrow causing his death. Achilles heel was his point of weakness and downfall. Homer's story parallels the human experience. It is painfully apparent that mankind has an Achilles' heel. A great mist has fallen. They are somehow clouded by their frazzled minds. There is a part of man that has not been baptized. There has been a mortal wound inflicted.

The heart of man is cold toward heaven's stage, and this condition has not improved with time. The fact that the Director's production is so well hidden from our daily dialogue begs the question, "What happened to man?" "Why are our hearts so cold?"

In *The Chronicles of Narnia*, the White Witch casts a spell over the land causing an endless season of snow. Narnia is held in the grip of her artic blast. Jadis, the White Witch, having killed her unnamed sister, now reigns over the hundred year winter. In *Frozen*, Elsa has used her icy powers to trap the kingdom of Arendelle in an eternal winter. Her heart refuses the reach of her sister, Anna. Fortunately, her sister and friends never gave up on her.

These stories mirror the coldness of the human heart, and our inability to break free from its grasp. From birth we have been frozen in our tracks. Locked in an ice chest we cannot open; frost has formed on our eyelids. The answer to this chilling dilemma lies long ago in a faraway land, but unlike Elsa, this is no fairytale. This story is a real-life drama that was played out in a once beautiful world that became an icy landscape. Before our thaw can occur, we must understand a tale older than time.

The first two actors to enter earth's stage were Adam and Eve. They lived in a garden called Eden. Soon after their creation, they went off script, and as a result, plunged us all into a hopeless condition. God gave them one simple command; stay away from the tree of the knowledge of good and evil. They chose to disobey. As a result, their rebellious spirit was passed onto us in the form of a crippling DNA. We all enter life's stage with a distinct limp caused by a severe case of ingrown eyeballs. We stumble because we cannot see clearly. To state the fact flatly, we were born with an Archilles Heal called sin. By this one act, we all inherited this debilitating deficit from that first couple. Adam and Eve did more than simply reject a commandment; they rebelled against the love of their Creator. Their betrayal against infinite love became our love of self. Rather than enter the Playwright's story, humanity has become the star of its own show.

Subsequently, "*My* kingdom come; *my* will be done," is plastered across the marquee outside our dressing room. Our perception of God's hand in our daily lives finishes a distant second to a more pervasive narrative, namely our conviction that we are the main character in a drama wherein we decide its acts and scenes. Our rebellion is to such an extreme that we believe we determine our own destiny, quite apart from an absent Creator. We imagine that we choose our closing scene. As William Ernest Henley wrote, "I am the Master of my fate, the captain of my soul."[19]

Sin has caused us to become riveted on a self-absorbing, self-destructive plotline. Our stage has shrunk to a miniature of its original design. All other actors and actresses spin in an orbit around our shining star. Our own self-importance is clutched with a death grip. As a result of refusing to hand over our tiny script for our greater role in God's play, we struggle with the meaning of life and our true worth.

Carrying the wound of those original actors has darkened the stage lights so that we cannot see our lives properly. We fumble in a fog searching for direction. Constantly questioning our value, we dance to a yawning audience. We lack a sense of God's purpose for our lives. The heavenly box office awaits us, but our habitation in our present cardboard box keeps us in the shadows. Let us continue down this dark road that will lead us to light.

In our attempt to please others, we lose our own identity. We allow our fellow actors and actresses to evaluate our daily performance rather than the Director of heaven. On the flip side, judging ourselves by the performances of others causes us to feel inadequate and insecure. Paul wrote this to the Corinthians… "Not that we dare to classify or compare ourselves with some of those who are commending themselves. But when they measure themselves by one another and compare themselves with one another, they are without understanding."[20] We desperately need to see the grander stage of heaven. Alas, there are more stumbling blocks on earth's stage.

Our earth-bound vantage point leads us to believe that our daily performances are played out before an empty theater. We wonder if anyone appreciates our efforts. Moreover, the longer we live the fewer are the grand moments that marked our earlier years. With the passage of time, the bulbs that light up our name on the marquee are slowly burning out. Our lives slowly become a box office disaster leading us down a dark path. We sit alone in our dressing room and wonder how life has suddenly become so meaningless. Our supporting cast members slowly dwindle away until we are at last alone. The despair we feel can grow so deep that we question the value of going on in life. This leads us to the inevitable despair of questioning the purpose of our existence. Does our life matter, and who cares if we live or die? Relevance is a predatory beast.

Shakespeare writes concerning Hamlet's struggle with life.

To be, or not to be: that is the question:
Whether 'tis nobler in the mind to suffer
The slings and arrows of outrageous fortune,
Or to take arms against a sea of troubles,
And by opposing end them? To die: to sleep;
No more; and by a sleep to say we end
The heartache and the thousand natural shocks.
That Flesh is heir to? 'Tis a consummation
Devoutly to be wished. To die, to sleep,
To sleep, perchance to Dream; aye, there's the rub,

For in that sleep of death, what dreams may come,
When we have shuffled off this mortal coil,
Must give us pause.

(HAMLET ACT 3 SCENE1)

Hamlet surmises that the suffering of life is so great that who would willingly bear it. To live and continue to suffer, or die and end his heartache, is the dilemma in his mind. Should he simply become a wallflower on the stage of life or, rather, take up a sword and battle *the heartache in the thousand natural shocks of life*. Prince Hamlet sees the struggles of life lived out on a horizontal plain. He agrees with Solomon, "What does man gain by all the toil at which he toils under the sun?"[21]

Hamlet has felt life's deepest pain and has drained the cup of bitterness. He has stood before his own theater and watched it go up in flames. His only hesitation is that he does not know what to expect in the afterlife. Perhaps the *dreams* of his existence after death will be worse than what he is experiencing in this life. His lines are raw because life is raw.

Along with the *shocks* of life, the critics of this world can be brutal. A thick, black line is drawn through our name on the playbill by ruthless theatergoers who dismiss us when we don't meet their expectations. The hecklers in the nickel seats are relentless. Beginning at our earliest age, they cast a thumbs down on our performances. We can all remember stinging comments made as we sat at our desk in a second-grade classroom. "Look at his big ears." "How did she get the part in the play?" "He'll never be first-string."

Young hearts are tender and easily wounded. Those moments are welded into our memories leaving us unsure of ourselves as the curtain rises each day. In the eyes of others, we are never good enough; we have never done enough. Our insecurities grow with each negative review. To exasperate the misery, we are prone to believe the few who judge us rather than the many who applaud us. The whispers from the corner become megaphones drowning out the cries for an encore. It is painfully true that one negative critic is more powerful in our minds than a thousand fans.

Attempting to conform, rather than transform the world around us, our square peg never fits into the round holes of other people's expectations. We sense an emptiness regardless of our best performances. Even when no critic is present, we quickly become our own worst enemy. We set up a standard for ourselves that no one could achieve.

Hamlet's question, *to be or not to be*, is unfortunately based on the presupposition that there are only two options in life; live and suffer or die and sleep. He considers ending his life without the realization of a third possibility. His choices are limited because his perspective is earthbound. The Great Playwright of Heaven has a more satisfying conclusion to his dilemma. Join his cast and live a life saturated with faith in a God who cannot fail in his purposes for your part. Hamlet chooses to, "*bear those ills we have rather than fly to others that we do not know of.*" Certainly, a miserable existence at best. Behold, "*conscience makes cowards of us all.*"

The writings of Shakespeare reflect a realism wherein man's despair is the keynote, and his struggles become the theme of life. It is the same battle which waged war in the mind of Solomon in the book of Ecclesiastes, "Vanity of Vanities, says the Preacher, vanity of vanities! All is vanity."[22] The King of Israel concluded that life was an empty chasm of nothingness with no bottom. Having gained all that life could offer, he sunk down in a dark closet and wept.

The conquering Roman general, Lucius Septimius Severus, defeated his rivals and became emperor in AD 193. However, all the glories of Rome, with its power and majesty, left the man empty and disillusioned. In his book, *The Decline and Fall of the Roman Empire*, Edward Gibbons writes, "Fortune and merit had, from a humble station, elevated him to the first place among mankind. "He had been all things," as he said himself, "and all was of little value."[23]

Chambers writes, "Let a man face facts as they are, and pessimism is the only possible conclusion. Job is seeing things exactly as they are. A healthy-minded man bases his life on actual conditions but let him be hit by bereavement and when he has got beyond the noisy bit, and the blasphemous bit he will find as Job found that despair is the basis of human life unless a man accepts a revelation from God and enters the Kingdom of Jesus Christ."[24]

Job's faith was carried into the crucible of tragedy and heartbreak. His core beliefs were tested in the fire of adversity, and when he came out on the other side, he possessed a depth of belief that his short-sighted friends could not fathom. Choices are made in the midst of struggle and loss that define our future walk with God. We must either throw ourselves back on our rationale way of thinking or step ahead into a deeper trust in the Director. For Job, the best was yet to come as his story was far from over.

Conversely, Hamlet's struggle left out the possibility of a heavenly theater with God as the Director. He failed to look beyond the tiny audience of himself and the few fellow actors surrounding him. He refused to be swept up onto a higher stage and into a greater manuscript. He was hounded with a sense of smallness in the grand scheme of things. We woefully feel the same.

In comparison to the universe, our planet is a dot on a vast horizon. On this tiny spinning ball, we call earth, it appears as though we are but particles of dust floating in the breeze. As the old song goes, "all we are is dust in the wind."[25] Our individual lives seem incredibly insignificant when compared to the march of humanity and the grandeur of the galaxies. We are tiny foot soldiers in the presence of an army of generals. Unfortunately, this is the appraisal of our landlocked and earthbound minds.

As a result, we battle with the fear that our lives are as meaningless as a drop of rain in a vast ocean. We fail to understand that the sea of life is incomplete without our "drop of rain." We mistakenly believe that our part does not matter. We share life's stage with a vast host of fellow actors and actresses and see little change wrought by our lines. No one seems to be listening. We evaluate our impact and find little to show for our efforts. What possible difference have we made in the ripples produced by the tiny pebble of our lives?

Solomon, one of the wisest men who ever lived, stated, "What does man gain by all the toil that he toils under the sun. A generation goes, and a generation comes but the earth remains forever. What has been is what will be, and what has been done is what will be done, and there is nothing new under the sun."[26] Chambers writes, "Everything man has ever done is constantly being obliterated, everything a man fights for and lives for passes; he has so many years to live and then it is finished. This is neither fiction nor dumps. In true thinking of things as they are, there is always a bedrock of unmitigated sadness."[27] We know instinctively that we were created for the grand stage of divine purpose. We sense our present theater is much too small as we drag our heels throughout life. Meant to soar to the heights, we are stuck in the mud; unable to pull our feet from the suction of this world.

We were fashioned for beauty and purpose, but like a carriage horse, we trot along life's path with blinders. On one hand, we dream of achieving great things, and yet, we battle with remembering where we left our car keys. We envision empires built by our very hands in the same moment that the hammer hits our thumb. Deep in our minds we dream of the big stage, while we spend our days sweeping the back alley.

The disconnect between these two competing storylines is caused by opposing perspectives. The view from an anthill is much different than from an eagle's nest. We simply have not climbed high enough to see the Grand Director's design and our place on his stage. We desperately need to see our lives from a different viewpoint, a divine perch. Man's true value only comes into focus from the camera angle of heaven.

Mankind intrinsically knows he is destined to fly with the wings of an eagle, and yet, we spend our days clawing around the barnyard searching for our next worm to devour. Created with eternal value and worth, we live in a decaying world where everything is judged by our worst moment. One bad line and the audience heads for the exits. The boos from the balcony only confirm what we have always suspected; we will never be enough; we will never measure up. At our deepest core, we all battle with these two diametrically opposing narratives. Heaven claims us as eternally precious, and earth regards us as a disposable commodity. The former is a gift from our Creator, the latter is our default mode caused by sin. Behold, the paradoxical nature of life. There *is* an answer to man's dilemma.

When Jesus came, he announced that the Kingdom of God had arrived, and yet, in the end, the majority walked away unaffected. There was an initial buzz of activity and excitement, however, after he went back to heaven, the masses settled back down into their grinding routines. It is no different today. The possibility of a heavenly kingdom, invading our here and now, seems ludicrous in the chaos which marks our days. If there is such a kingdom in our midst, then why is there so much pain? The authorities that presently rule our world appear unaffected by the lonely Carpenter from Nazareth.

The key to gaining heaven's perspective is closer than we think. The answer to our Achilles' heel is staring us in our face. We must face the truth of our rebel heart and yield to the Great Director. This involves a decision prompted by the will. Faith in Christ to be our Redeemer is the answer to our Achilles' heel of sin. Once we cross that river of redemption, we begin to look beyond ourselves and unto Jesus. As we seek his will, not our own, we begin to move on God's great dance floor. "But seek first the kingdom of God and his righteousness, and all these things will be added to you."[28] The limp that marked our days vanishes with each new verse and chorus. The path becomes clear, and our stride becomes sure and true. Surrender is the keynote in the orchestra pit of glory. It is only at this point that the great journey begins.

The path will then become clearer each day as we march to Zion. Some changes will not happen overnight, but they will come to pass. We will fly on eagles' wings even though now we may appear to be roosting in an old, broken-down hen house. Alen Redpath, a British pastor once wrote, "The conversion of a soul is the miracle of a moment, the manufacture of a saint is the task of a lifetime."[29] Just wait for it; he will not disappoint us.

We have been conditioned for so long to swallow the lie that he doesn't truly love us. Our minds will deceive us into thinking that God is only interested in what we can do for him, or that he wants to keep us under his thumb. It is our hearts, not our minds, that must choose to receive the truth of God's unconditional love. Solomon wrote, "He has made everything beautiful in its time. Also, he has put eternity into man's heart, yet so that he cannot find out what God has done from the beginning to the end."[30] The mystery of his workings are beyond our comprehending, and yet, he has promised a beautiful ending for the redeemed. He creates beauty out of ashes and builds on top of the ruins of our lives. As he did when he created our world, he hovers over our dark waters and declares,

"Let there be light." We were without form and void before the Playwright appeared.

Heaven's stage is not up yonder but is found in the mix of life in this present world. Juvenal, the Roman satirist, wrote, "All of Greece is a stage, and every Greek an actor."[31] These ancient men of the Acropolis understood they were part of a great drama, an ongoing production if you will. Telling stories were their forte while living in the shadowy realm of their present world. Plato believed that every earthly object had its heavenly twin. Every nook and cranny held a thousand gods who could surprise and shock them at any given moment. While Plato was wrong in believing that there were many gods, the thought of heaven's stage, right outside his doorstep, was and is still true. We resign ourselves to a life of mediocrity by ignoring the reality of God's greater drama. As Plato wrote, "We can easily forgive a child who is afraid of the dark; the real tragedy of life is when men are afraid of the light."[32]

The painful existence of man is fully realized in his futile attempt to find light in the darkness of his mind. Determined to carve out a path of his own choosing he keeps falling into the same ditch over and over again. He is like a blind man looking in a dark room for a black cat that isn't there. Paul wrote, "They are darkened in their understanding, alienated from the life of God because of the ignorance that is in them, due to their hardness of heart."[33] When Jesus came, he brought light into a dark world. His Shekinah glory still beams out into the blackness of mankind calling for a decision. "In him was life, and the life was the light of men. The light shines in the darkness, and the darkness has not overcome it."[34]

God is the great Playwright, and his stage has been set from eternity past. The Director is busy directing his masterpiece and bringing his tale of redemption to a magnificent conclusion. The question remains what part you will choose to play. To launch out into the great adventure of God rather than chasing your own empty dreams seems like an easy decision, but it is not. Choosing light over darkness involves rejecting our own sovereignty for his Kingship. And he said to all, "If anyone would come after me, let him deny himself and take up his cross daily and follow me."[35]

Regardless, we all will play a part in the ongoing drama of the redemptive narrative. Pharaoh, as well as Moses, told the story of the Exodus.

Moreover, the heavenly theater is packed out. The audience may appear thin down here, but on a higher plain the playhouse is filled to capacity. We may not see the filled seats, but they are warmed by the heavenly host. The stage awaits your entrance as the angels sit in anticipation. To miss this great saga is to stand outside the playhouse looking miserably through fogged-glassed windows and wonder why you exist. To embrace heaven's stage is to discover the true meaning of life and to look forward to eternity.

Jesus said, "Fear not, little flock, for it is your Father's good pleasure to give you the kingdom."[36] This present life is simply a prologue to a never-ending story. Let's open the manuscript and begin to see that our lives are not our own and that he has always been present. His plans for us are greater than we can imagine, with twists and turns that will keep us on the edge of our seats.

CHAPTER 3

The manuscript

O scar Hammerstein II was born in 1895. He rose to fame as a lyrist, writing such works as *Oklahoma, South Pacific*, and *The Sound of Music*. His collaborations with Richard Rodgers produced some of the most amazing productions of the last century. Composer Johnny Green called Oscar, "a businessman-poet," and Rodgers described his partner as, "a dreamer, but a very careful dreamer."

Todd S. Purdum, in his book, *Something Wonderful*, describes the moment Hammerstein discovered the theater would be his future. "Later, alone in the dark theater, young Oscar watched transfixed as a bevy of women, costumed as water maidens, sought to untangle a large fishing net, and sang a beguiling siren song. At intermission, his father took him backstage, where he promptly came face-to-face with a large lion in a cage. Suddenly the cage started to roll toward him, and he feared he might be sick to his stomach. By one later account, he went home, slept fourteen hours, and 'when he awoke, he announced that the theater would be his life's work.'"[37]

Hammerstein eventually became a playwright, producer, and director, serving the musical industry for nearly forty years. His focus on stories, brought to life by memorable characters, replaced the lighthearted entertainment that had previously dominated the stage. In essence, he was devoted to the idea of a manuscript. The fire that burned within

Hammerstein was but a reflection of the great Playwright of heaven who is still telling his story through men and women today.

By definition a manuscript is a hand-written document or writing that has not yet gone to publication. It is by its very nature a work in close proximity to its author. An intimate relationship exists between a writer and what he has written. Laboring away in quietness, the writer collects his thoughts and then creates storylines with characters and context. The plot must develop naturally with flowing narrative and lively dialogue. The reader must feel the mist lifting from the bay or the blast of artic air on a frozen tundra. Rising action must lead to a dramatic climax followed by falling action, and then, of course, resolution. Once his scribblings are finished, the author sends his manuscript off to be published, kissing his 'baby' farewell. With a tear in his eye, emptiness fills him. Writing is personal.

Likewise, God has penned a manuscript concerning mankind that is very personal to him. His story contains all the elements listed above except for a few differences. Unlike the writings of men, his is a breathing, living document revealing his masterful fullness and beauty. Also, God doesn't send his story to a publisher and then walk away. He stays intimately involved as the chapters unfold. His manuscript is written in heaven and played out among the sons of men.

Our lives begin in earnest when we realize that our individual stories are embedded in a grander theme. Our names are included in his manuscript. Our lives are more than just shooting stars which dissolve into space. Life is filled with the destiny God has planned for each one of us. The stormy days, as well as those bathed in sunlight, are all a part of his plan. Realizing this truth breathes meaning into every pothole of life. It gives us confidence to keep traveling forward toward that heavenly city. There is purpose in the nuances of life.

The Playwright has also been weaving our lives with those all around us, and his plans were set in motion long before we were born. When we enter heaven's stage, we realize that there is a part to be played, and epic does not begin to describe what God has penned for our ever-expanding, changing character.

In the passing of ordinary days, it is easy to lose track of this truth. We are driven to distraction by the temporal while the eternal is staring us in the face. We ignore the elephant of the everlasting and focus on the gnat of now. We forget that our lives have meaning beyond our present horizon. Pestered by a thousand worrisome mosquitos, we agree with Solomon, "All things are full of weariness; a man cannot utter it; the eye is not satisfied with seeing, nor the ear filled with hearing."[38] But life is more than just passing time while we wait for the grave. There are dragons to be slayed and lands to be conquered. The great manuscript of God awaits us.

When I was a young boy, my father would always introduce me as his, "little preacher." I would smile and think to myself, *how does he know that?* As I grew older and became involved in some youthful indiscretions, I would think, *he really doesn't know me very well.* However, he apparently knew me better than I knew myself, as I have been pastoring now for many years. I've made choices in life, but ultimately, God's hand was the guiding factor.

The Playwright knows us intimately and writes our character accordingly. Jesus saw Nathanael coming toward him and said, "Behold, an Israelite indeed, in whom there is no deceit!" Nathanael asked, "How do you know me?" Jesus answered, "Before Philip called you, when you were under the fig tree, I saw you."[39] There is nothing more ordinary than standing under a tree, and yet, that's where Philip was called. Jesus doesn't need a grand cathedral or blazing sunset to get our attention. He is in the simple, daily, shade tree moments.

Take time to think deeply concerning the movements of your life in concert with the Playwright of heaven, and you may discover a pattern. You may see that the sharp bends in the road were meant to steer you toward Jesus. It all becomes clear when we step back. Consequently, to be filled with regrets for past mistakes is to doubt his plan. Wishing life had turned out differently is to squander today and lose a perspective for the future. Seeing life from God's vantage point rather than a narrow focus changes things. It is sometimes difficult to see the forest from the trees, but the forest is there, and it is filled with his story. Tree hugging our individual problems will only smear our faces with pine sap. Stepping back and looking out into a fresh pine forest of a new day is what fills his manuscript.

In writing his personal memoirs, Ulysses S. Grant included this well-worn, pithy statement, "Man proposes but God disposes." Grant goes on to pen this profound analysis, "There are but few important events in the affairs of men brought about by their own choice." The entirety of Grant's life revealed the divine hand of Providence in his every move. As a backwoods boy from Pleasant Point, Ohio, he was thrust onto the national stage as the victorious General of the Northern Armies. Howbeit, between those two events were many dark and confusing days in which the future hero of the Union forces had no idea where his life would finish.

In December 1862, when malaria and smallpox broke out among the troops, Grant was questioned by the Northern Press concerning the sanitary conditions in his camp. Even though the illnesses were well contained, the newspapers exaggerated the situation to cast doubt on Grant's ability to lead the North. As his army waited for the winter rains to recede, the General remained silent. His leadership was assailed with vicious attacks. He writes, "Because I would not divulge my ultimate plans to visitors, they pronounced me to be idle, incompetent and unfit to command men in an emergency, and clambered for my removal."[40] The press even went as far as to suggest his replacement.

Grant's reaction reveals a man at rest with the hand of God on his life. He writes, "Everyone has his superstitions. One of mine is that in positions of great responsibility everyone should do his duty to the best of his ability, where assigned by competent authority, without application or the use of influence to change his position."[41] He was a man who waited on the right moment to act. On one occasion, as the cavalry was advancing into an important battle, a soldier named Captain Hillyer suggested to Grant to command the charge. Grant replied, "I then told him that I would cut my right arm off first and mentioned my superstition."[42]

Grant acknowledged the fact that life brings with it a strong current, carrying us to distant shores, and then thrusting us into exploits and adventures we would have never chosen for ourselves. Dying of cancer, he sat on a porch in upstate New York and wrote the story of his life as he saw it. Looking back, he quietly reflected on the great and small movements of his life that were profoundly beyond his control but fully in the power of the Playwright. Providence was at work as he acknowledged at the end of his life.

Imagine for a moment that you, as an actor or actress, receive a manuscript for the first time. With bated breath, you search to find your part in the play. The thrill of being included in the performance is suddenly replaced by the anxiety of wondering if it's the right role for you. You wonder if you have what it takes to fill the part. You scan the list of fellow actors and actresses to see if you are a good fit. You hope that the role will advance your career and seal your place on theater's golden stage. You are keenly aware that the graveyard awaits the thespian who is repeatedly cast in disastrous productions. How long will the play run and will all the sacrifice be worth your time and effort. The decision to join the cast is firmly in your court. The casting director waits for your response. The invitation to enter the Director's production on heaven's stage is much different.

First of all, you are not handed a script or even told who your character will be in the story. You are not asked to memorize lines or to portray a persona that is foreign to your personality. Authenticity with your own personality is the key to success. In other words, you are asked by the Director to simply be yourself. In fact, you do not *play* a part, you *are* the part.

Furthermore, your fellow actors and actresses show up on each day of the performance unannounced. Some are regulars, while others are new to the mix, and you have no idea how long you will share a stage with any of them. The casting director substitutes actors and actresses at will, without your approval or consent. Fellow actors, whom you have shared a stage with for years, are sometimes permanently removed, leaving you bewildered and angry. Some fellow actors stay long after you wish they would depart.

Moreover, new lines are delivered to your dressing room moments before the curtain goes up, and sometimes, you don't even get that much notice. It is useless to suggest a certain storyline as the Director seems determined to tell each day's adventure in his own way and with his own timing. He keeps you off balance with scenes that do not seem to connect and with strange characters who defy reasonable inclusion in the overall story. Heaven's stage is wildly unpredictable, yet deeply satisfying.

Imagine the first time that the disciples gathered around Jesus. No doubt there were some long looks and quick, premature judgements. None of them knew what to expect, but one thing would become crystal clear, they were in for a wild ride. Plot twists were thrust upon them without warning and sometimes in devastating ways. There were countless days when they looked back, and nothing seemed to make sense. Months flew by being filled with nonsensible rollercoaster narratives. Life swirled at a speed that made their heads spin and sent them crashing into their tents each evening exhausted and bewildered.

What happened to the disciples is true in our own walk with the Master. Shakespeare called this phenomenon, "the slings and arrows of outrageous Fortune."[43] The loss of a job, the sudden death of a loved one, or an unexpected illness arrives at our doorstep. Bumpety bump goes life along a very rough road. Try as we might, we fail to make sense of the Director's confusing manuscript. There is more to consider.

When a playwright sends out a script to an acting group, he or she expects it to be followed down to every jot and tittle. Backdrops, props, and music are written into the manuscript to set a mood, preparing the audience for the story that will unfold. Dramatic lines, along with comic relief, are carefully placed so that the play flows just as the playwright desired. Every line matters and every movement counts. Like steps on a ladder, the writer connects scenes and characters in such a way so that the audience will reach the pinnacle of the story and be gripped by its message. Storylines build with rising action called crescendos leading to the inevitable climax of the tale. Falling action brings resolution, and the story is complete.

Without adhering carefully to the script, the story fails its intended purpose. Regardless of lines delivered, if those lines are not in the manuscript, they detract and sometimes ruin the story being told. The actors must honor the playwright by their adherence to the script.

My good friend, Jay Huling, is a playwright. He travels around the country to sit in audiences and view the plays he has written. The aim of the theater group is to tell the tale just as Jay intended. The personalities of the actors in each theater certainly add color to the scenes, but regardless, the playwright wants his story to be told just as he wrote it.

Within the rolling history of mankind even the timing of our birth has been crucial to the overarching story. Those who love history often wonder what it would have been like to be born in another time period. Men fantasize of chopping wood with Abraham Lincoln or marching into battle with William Wallace. Women dream of living out their lives in the simplicity and safety of the 1950's or marching for the right to vote. However, whether we were born in the first chapter of the manuscript, or the last, it is all the Playwright's choosing. Our birth launched us onto life's stage right on cue to fulfill very specific moments, and those moments come to us every day.

It is doubtful that our name will ever make it into a history book, but that does not matter. Our life's story is orchestrated by the very hand of the Director, not with the pen of any earthly historian. On the pages of glory's eternal record, every name in the story will appear. Furthermore, the evil plans of men cannot hinder God's plan for our lives. God keeps writing our saga despite Satan's effort to hit the delete button. No one makes changes to the manuscript. "Man proposes but God disposes." We chart out our lives and then God sends a west wind and blows us in a new and unexpected direction.

The story of our lives also includes fellow characters that are as different from us as corn and silk. At times, we may question why we share the stage with those with whom we have little in common. We must keep in mind that the ability to create a lively story is contingent on our dissimilarities. Differing personalities are the very thing that give a play color and interest. Where would Elizabeth Bennet be without Fitzwilliam Darcy? There is no Odysseus without Penelope, no Batman without Robin, and no Pumbaa without Timon. Time fails me to mention Abbott and Costello or Laurel and Hardy. The Lone Ranger trotting off into the sunset without Tonto is a sad scene. If two actors on the stage are similar then one is not needed. Consequently, it is important to simply be ourselves, regardless of what that looks like.

Likewise, often what we see within ourselves as a defect God deems beautiful. We hide our weaknesses while the Director uses them as a crowning jewel. The short stature of Zacchaeus put him in a sycamore tree. The big mouth of Peter was used on the day of Pentecost. Rahab the harlot hid the Israelites who came to spy out the land, and the fiery temper of Martin Luther ignited the Great Reformation. Augustine's great struggle with sin caused him to embrace and understand grace. That which we think excludes us actually qualifies us to be in God's great production. Perfect faces and sculptured bodies are for mannikins, not real people. Lives that have been untouched by the rugged realities of life need not apply. Birthmarks are the kiss of an angel, and deformities are embraced on heaven's stage.

We are also drawn to those who do not seek to hide their struggles and insecurities. Character flaws are what make characters relatable and good stories become epic tales when God enters the scene. The church at Corinth was told to look around and see who was sitting next to them in the pew. Not many rich and powerful filled the church. God has chosen the foolish and weak of this world to confound the mighty.[44]

Even those born with physical and mental challenges are seen on heaven's stage as a gift from God, as a dear friend recently suggested. Those who have raised children with Down Syndrome testify to the blessedness of those children. A child with autism needs the love and understanding of those who encircle them. It is a great privilege to be trusted by the Lord to nurture those little ones placed under our care. James wrote that God has chosen the poor of this world to be rich in faith. I had the privilege of knowing a dear lady named Anna. For many years she struggled with physical and mental challenges. She is now safely in heaven with a clear mind and a healthy body. Anna is worshiping her Savior. God makes no mistakes. In the end, our frailties are really beautiful birthmarks, marking us out as cast members in his story.

Consequently, it is the humble that he uses on his stage. George Washington, in a letter to his wife Martha, wrote this regarding his future as the General of the Continental Army, "far from seeking this appointment, I have used every endeavor in my power to avoid it, not only for my unwillingness to part with you and the family, but from a consciousness of its being a trust too great for my capacity... it has been a kind of destiny that has thrown me upon this service."[45] He understood the sacrifice needed to lead the effort to break free from England, and his shortcomings in the accomplishment of that great feat. As history unfolded, he proved to be the man for the hour.

There are also no flat characters in his script and no stationary wall flowers. Even those who do play a part as a motionless tree or a silent cabbage are celebrated with great fervor. Every actor on heaven's stage holds equal force and presence. There are no leading roles or supporting actresses. All the parts and lines are vital to the overall story. In the final curtain call, all the actors and actresses come out at the same time. On heaven's stage all the cast receives the same thunderous applause and standing ovations. Cries for an encore are directed to the cast as a whole. We will stand one day next to Moses and Paul receiving the same recognition. Faithfulness to the role he has given is the only standard. All the stage performers, though diverse and unique from one another, receive equal accolades. He will exclaim for all to hear, "Well done, thou good and faithful servant."

The Author who wrote you into his story is excited about every day you live because your life enriches his saga. He is fully invested on giving you an expected end, a glorious finale. You may think that your life carries with it the taste of vanilla and that your days are filled with a series of meaningless events followed by the sleepy yawns of friends and family, but you would be wrong. There is not a day of your life that is not jam-packed with the Director's purposes for you. He is behind every detail of your life, working out his script. Even though you may not see him, he sees you.

The name of God is not mentioned once in the book of Esther, and yet, his fingerprints are all over the story. King Xerxes's decision to remove Vashti paved the way for Esther's place in the palace and eventually into his heart. The Persian King's rash decision to destroy the Jewish people forced Esther to plead for the life of her people. Esther's entire life was a preparation for that singular event. Her Uncle Mordecai reminded her that perhaps, "she has been born for such a time as this."[46] It was her moment to step out onto the stage apron and fulfill the heartbeat of the Playwright. Esther's abandonment to the script was evident in her cry, "if I die, I die."[47] Mordecai watched as the evil Haman hung from the very gallows that had been built for him.

Before David became a king, he was a shepherd. No doubt, to a young lad watching over a flock of sheep, the experience was an exercise in extreme boredom. Hour upon hour, he spent looking over the hills, watching for dangers that hardly ever came. To make matters worse, rams and ewes are boring creatures. Sheep are never found in a three-ring circus. They chew on grass, wander off, and get stuck on rock ledges. Their constant bleating can drive a man mad, and yet, David endured the drudgery. In his patience and commitment, he discovered that the Great Shepherd was like a shepherd to him. He also learned how to kill a giant with a sling and a stone. Those lonely nights sitting on a hillside were not wasted in the life of the future King of Israel. Those experiences tested his resolve to stay at the task. Chambers stated, "It is one thing to go through a crisis grandly, but a different thing to go through everyday glorifying God when there is no witness, no limelight, and no one paying the remotest attention to you."[48]

The lilies that bloom in a hidden forest, unseen, still display God's glory. They spring up unexpectedly with the early rains and then taste the dryness of death. They are like people who are pushed into the cracks of life and forgotten. Before Romeo became heart-smitten for Juliet, he was love-struck with her cousin, Rosaline. When Romeo gazed into Rosaline's eyes there could be no other, "The all-seeing sun / ne'er saw her match since first the world begun." (Romeo and Juliet 1.2/99-100) However, after spotting Juliet at a gathering, Romeo's heart was bewitched. His love for Rosaline was but a steppingstone to Juliet. Tragic for the former, and still more tragic for the latter. No one remembers poor Rosaline, but alas, she played a significant part in the most famous love story of all time.

In the mundane he is preparing us to face giants. Rest comes to the soul who understands this truth. After the miraculous birth in Bethlehem, Jesus lived an ordinary childhood. On the heels of the Transfiguration, Jesus walked into a demon-filled situation at the base of the mountain. Following the resurrection, the Master met his men on the sea of Galilee for a morning breakfast. We crave for the spectacular while he walks with us through ordinary days.

The kindness of the Scriptwriter is directing our lives to its ultimate fulfillment even though we do not know our next line or scene. As the story of the Playwright is swirling all around us, we must grab the bull by the horns and hang on for dear life. Our only responsibility is keeping our eyes on the Director and being ready for his next cue. Living in the moment, in all its gusto, is the goal.

Jackie Gleason never rehearsed more than a few times before he taped live episodes on, *The Honeymooners*. He wanted each scene to feel fresh and alive with spontaneity. Gleason rejected a canned and rehearsed show. Every new day is an unfolding adventure where the ink on the script is still wet. The Director's theater is the ultimate impromptu venue. The Playwright is passionately routing for your success. He celebrates every moment of your performance. The prophet Jeremiah wrote, "For I know the thoughts that I think toward you, saith the Lord, thoughts of peace, and not of evil, to give you an expected end."[49] The Lord is not hiding behind the next tree waiting to crush your performance. He has written a marvelous manuscript with a part custom-made for you.

In a very real sense, our lives are stories. As each new day dawns, another chapter begins. As the ink dries with each setting sun, the tale of that day is recorded in the eternal record. After the curtain falls, we can neither add to it, nor erase what has been said or done. Days may appear like a long string of disconnected short stories lacking cohesiveness, and some may even feel like the end of the road. However, there is more going on in our lives than we can presently understand. We are all victims of the short view.

Jesus said that a sparrow does not fall to the ground without his Father knowing it. He also stated that the very hairs of our head are numbered. These small details in the natural realm seem unimportant, but not to the Creator. Jesus told us about these things for a specific reason. If he guides the wings of a small bird, he is also aware of our every step. If he numbers our hair follicles, he cares about every detail of our lives. The force and speed of life can strip this simple truth from our perspective. It is easy to forget how intimately involved he is in every punctuation point of our days.

It is life's greatest privilege to be included in his manuscript. We silently long to be remembered by men, but the true tale of the ages flows from the pen of the Playwright. He alone writes the stories that will be eternally recorded. Daniel wrote, "And those who are wise shall shine like the brightness of the sky above; and those who turn many to righteousness, like the stars forever and ever."[50] God's reward is not a trophy that will rust or can be stolen. His accolades are everlasting, and the laurels we shall receive will never wither with the hot blow of an east wind. His hand-written manuscript is the tale of our lives and our opportunity to bring glory to his name.

CHAPTER 4

Casting Call

George Cukor knew immediately that Vivian Leigh was the right choice to cast as Scarlett O'Hara in the Oscar award winning movie, *Gone with the Wind*. He and David O Selznick met the British actress on the movie set of *The Burning of Atlanta* on December 10, 1938, and were enthralled. Cukor told *The Atlantic* years later that she was, "charged with electricity' and "possessed of the devil." Critics, though, were not happy with his pick. Leigh was neither a southerner nor was she even an American. Hedda Hopper, a gossip columnist of the time wrote this, "Mr. Selznick was two years deciding on his Scarlet, and out of millions of American women couldn't find one to suit him."[51] She predicted people would stay home, and yet, the movie went on to be the highest grossing film in its day. Close to 1400 women were interviewed, and in the end, Vivian Leigh prevailed to become the celebrated vixen of The Twelve Oaks. She had the right look, the perfect temperament, and she was a force to be reckoned with in dealing with the likes of Rhett Butler.

Casting is crucial to the success of any production. The moment a character steps onto the stage a mental image is cast into the mind of the audience, and it is vital that the actor or actress fits the bill. Plots are driven by narrative, dialog, and the persona of each performer. A harsh line delivered by a soft voice is not believable. Scar Face crooning under an autumn moon to his lover leaves those sitting in the audience with serious questions. George Baily burning down Old Man Potter's bank in a fit of rage makes you wonder if he really did have a wonderful life. We need the brashness of Scar Face and the calm demeanor of George Baily seen in the faces of the men who played those parts. Each part must be performed in a convincing manner by the right person who sets the right tone for the part. We want to be drawn into the plot by fascinating, compelling characters. A good director will search long and hard to make sure that each part is filled by the right person. Casting is crucial.

Likewise, in the Director's story of redemption, our distinct personalities, intellect, as well as our physical attributes, were crafted for the part we are to play. Long before the flower ever opens, the bud holds all the particulars of its anticipated beauty and purpose. It only needs soil, sunlight, and rain to realize its destiny. Those elements are found on heaven's stage in the Director himself.

God made no mistake concerning the life he has placed within us. King David declared, "My frame was not hidden from you, when I was being made in secret, intricately woven in the depths of the earth."[52] David celebrated the fact that he was made in the image of God and that his Creator was intimately involved in the crafting process. His soul was convinced that his life had intrinsic value, and his heart sang for joy. He knew that he was groomed in the womb for his moment in the spotlight. Every single part of our pre-birth preparation was vital to our story. We are all unique, and yet, we are all, "fearfully and wonderfully made." God's handiwork is perfect.

Consequently, diversity is the joy-filled expression of the Creator. A cookie cutter cast is a dull performance at best. Uniformity within humanity is the antithesis of divine creativity, and so, our distinctions as human beings are exactly what the script of heaven needs. He uses every color in his painting palate to complete his masterpiece. Every personality and quirk of human nature is written into the script. Men would divide us by our differences, while the Playwright uses those same distinctions to unite us for a common purpose. A quilt is made beautiful by a master quilt-maker's ability to blend colors and designs together as one seamless tapestry. There is beauty in every human being.

The Apostles were as different as they could be, and yet, he chose them to form a cohesive band of followers. In any other setting, Simon the Zealot would have had nothing to do with Matthew the tax collector. Peter, the loudmouth fisherman, would have dismissed John for being so quiet. Apart from Jesus, these men and women would have bounced off each other like marbles, but instead, they meshed like a bag of soft grapes. It was the power of his life among them that made the difference.

Furthermore, the Director of the play is unseen, and yet, he occupies a chair that pilots 360. He is ever-present in all his fullness. God knows all about the itch before we think to scratch. Throughout the ongoing menagerie of human activity, he is also at work, and most of the time we are unaware he is directing us. There is not a movement he misses as millions live out their lives before him. While weaving the actors and actresses together, he flawlessly intertwines them into the fabric of life.

Also, we are not allowed to read over our part, and so, we have no idea how any particular issue will end. As much as we would like to see the last line of the play, it is hidden from view. On any given day the final curtain may drop as we clutch our chest and take our last breath. "In the day of prosperity be joyful, and in the day of adversity consider God has made the one as well as the other, so that man may not find out anything that will be after him."[53] To top it all off, we are asked to pledge our undying loyalty to the production. We are expected to deeply trust the guiding hand of the Lord.

Heaven's stage is beyond anything we can comprehend or imagine. Isaiah's quill recorded the Lord's mind when he wrote, "For my thoughts are not your thoughts, neither are your ways my ways, declares the Lord. For as the heavens are higher than the earth so are my ways higher than your ways and my thoughts than your thoughts."[54] Perhaps we should take a step back, catch our breath, and get a new perspective of heaven's theater and even more importantly, his methods. In receiving the call, it is vital we understand the Director and the story he is telling. This alone will help us understand and appreciate our part in the ongoing drama.

The very first verse in the Bible declares, "In the beginning God created..."[55] This simple statement tells us something very important about the Director. He is the origin and the starting place for everything done under the sun. He is square one for all things as it relates to his story. Nothing happens without his initiative. The Playwright originates; we participate. He is the "First Cause; the Unmovable Mover," as the Greek philosopher Aristotle is recorded to have said. Jesus taught that a sparrow does not fall to the ground without the Heavenly Father knowing it. The fall leaves change on his command and display the colors of his choosing. The first spring bud appears on the sugar maple on his timetable. Our lives bring fruit when he ordains it to be so and not before. All things come to pass at his pleasure.

The Lord is also firmly in control of his story, and he is flawless in its delivery. What we view is a discombobulated mess, he sees as poetic perfection. He brings beauty out of ashes. He sits back in his chair each morning, and with a wave of his hand, along with the megaphone of heaven, he cries action. The heroes along with the villains are woven together in seamless narratives producing a flowing drama. Perfectly mixing the free will of the actors and actresses with his directive cues, he accomplishes his purposes, and so, he is never surprised with the outcome. Those who truly believe he is in control rest in the chaos.

Solomon made this observation, "Consider the work of God: who can make straight what he has made crooked?"[56] It is, of course, a rhetorical question meant to reveal the truth of our inability to control circumstances. The answer is no one can corral the wind or stop an incoming tide. Each day presents itself with endless interruptions with unexpected twists and turns. Plan out your day all you want and watch the Director ignore your script. Sip your coffee in the calm of the morning and strategize the next twelve hours. Plan on a fun day at the beach with the family, and you will end up getting your truck stuck in the sand. Make the day as straight as you can, and as the sun goes down, you will look back and see how crooked it became. As the poet Robert Burns once wrote, "The best laid plans of mice and men often go awry."[57]

The Lord is closer than our breath. Only the Director can mix an impromptu format with a structured script design. He is intensely involved in each scene, and he has done this effortlessly since the beginning of time. Simply put, God is always working all things according to his glorious timeline.

It is also encouraging to note that he never regrets calling us to be a part of his story. Paul states, "His gifts and calling are without repentance."[58] He is never sorry he chose us to be a part of his production. The Lord will never repent of the day when he dialed us up for the golden stage. No matter how many mistakes we make, he will never stomp out of the theater while tossing the script into the nearest trash can. The pages of the manuscript never fly into the air having been thrown into empty seats because he became frustrated.

As a young boy, I learned an important lesson from my mother regarding forgiveness and grace. I was in first grade, and apparently, I had been misbehaving in class. Having been sent out of the room, I sat alone on a stoop waiting for the class to be dismissed. I had forgotten, though, that my mother was coming to eat lunch with me that day. Up to that point, I had felt no particular shame or remorse for my behavior, but when I saw mom walking down the hallway, my heart sank. Anxiety grew as I heard her approaching footsteps. To my surprise, she never said a word. She simply walked up and sat down next to me. We waited in silence until the class was over and then went to lunch together. I never received a word of rebuke or displeasure for my scandalous behavior. My mother wisely knew there would be another day to prove myself and that her son was suffering shame enough in the moment. Grace had won the day.

Likewise, the Director is not disappointed in a bad scene. He sits down next to us and simply responds, "What's done is done. Let's move onto the next scene." There is no need to spin our wheels in the mud of regret when God has placed our feet on the solid rock of his forgiveness. We do him the greatest honor by launching ourselves into the next scene with a clear conscience. To drag our feet, when we should be running into his arms, is to doubt the power of the blood he gave to make us holy.

On the night Jesus was betrayed, all his disciples tucked tail and ran. He had predicted they would abandon him. His insistence that *all* would deny him was met with resistance by Peter. Pointing at the other disciples, Peter assured Jesus that even though they all walked away, he would stand firm to the end, even unto death. The big, bold, self-confident fisherman fell hard that night, and Jesus was there to pick him up after the resurrection. Paul records a private meeting between Jesus and Peter in his letter to the Corinthians. The words spoken between them will forever be private, but we know Peter was restored back to heaven's stage. On the day of Pentecost, when the Holy Spirit arrived, it was the three-time denier from Galilee who preached to thousands in Jerusalem. The grace of God, being communicated through vessels of clay, would become the model of the church. Flawed actors and actresses belting out the tunes and hitting their lines came to be the modus operandi; the standard mode of operation. The Director is pleased with his wounded and weary artists.

Jesus instructed them to meet him in Galilee after his resurrection. The fact that they were all going to run when the heat was turned up did not deter his plan for using them to reach the world with the truth. In fact, they were all better prepared to preach grace after having received it themselves. He does the same with us.

From the Bible's perspective, the Playwright delights in using the outcast and the fallen. Moses was a murderer. Abraham was an idol worshipper. Eve bit the forbidden fruit and Adam followed. Noah got drunk and lay naked in a cave. King David committed adultery and then had Bathsheba's husband killed to cover the fact of her pregnancy. Matthew chose a profession of treason against his own people. Simon the Zealot was a political revolutionary willing to kill any Roman in his way. Peter couldn't keep his mouth shut long enough to tie his sandals. Mary Magdalene was a woman with a checkered past. Paul actively imprisoned Christians and orchestrated the death of the church's first martyr, Stephen.

It is interesting that the Bible never attempts to hide these failures and flaws. The lives of the great saints, throughout the ages, have always been on display, warts, and all. Augustine struggled with immorality. Martin Luther battled depression. The list goes on and on, but none of these self-inflicted wounds kept the Director from calling these men and women into his story and changing them by the tale being told. This is his method on heaven's stage.

Novels or plays fall into one of two categories. They are either plot-driven or character-driven. In other words, the story is either about the characters and their development, or the plot, and the characters are simply there to move the story along. Charles Dickens's classic, *David Copperfield,* is an example of a character-driven novel. The story of Copperfield's struggles and ultimate triumph fills the pages of the novel. Dan Brown's, *The da Vinci Code,* is a classic plot-driven story. A cryptic code placed into a work of Leonardo da Vinci is the centerpiece of Brown's thriller. Playwrights are constrained to one of these two methods.

However, on heaven's stage both methods are active. The Director's story is both character-driven and plot-driven. The development of his sons and daughters moves his plot forward. He cares as much about his actors and actresses as the story he wants to tell through them. He fashions us for entrances and exits in the ongoing scenes of his narrative. The grand story is both external and internal to the performers who dance and sing with intrinsic passion. Discourses are rendered, monologues uttered, complete with body language and inflection, all to fulfill his purposes. These elements are a result of the people we are becoming on a daily basis.

Within the world of psychology, there is an age-old debate regarding the place that nature plays in our development as human beings versus the impact that proper nurturing has in the crucial stages in our lives. In other words, are we the product of our heredity or does our life's experiences guide our journey? Unfortunately, it is often presented as an either-or proposition.

There is little doubt that the characteristics of our ancestors have been indelibly etched into our DNA. We can easily see our face in the face of our great grandfather or grandmother. Those old pictures are like looking into a mirror, but the similarities go far beyond appearances. The internal grit and gristle of our lives have been passed down to us from the people who went before us in our bloodline. One of my ancestors was a Puritan preacher who, with his own hands, built a church in the wilderness of Connecticut in the 1600s. I think of that when I'm working at the church. Maybe not the same thing but close enough to make me smile.

It is also undeniable that what we encounter in life changes us. Whether we were raised in a home that resembled the Little House on the Prairie, or Nightmare on Elm Street, either experience impacted us. We don't get kicked in the mouth without losing a few teeth nor do we have a warm blanket wrapped around us without feeling comforted. So, which of these two factors determines our place on the stage of heaven? Actually, the answer is both. It is the blending of these two elements by the Playwright which steers us toward our dressing room and out onto the stage.

Yet, there is a third angle to consider. Ultimately, it is our personal decisions in life that tells the evitable tale of intrigue and suspense. We are not victims in life, confined to genetics or a rough start. God has given us a will to decide the direction of our lives. Confronted with the claims of Jesus Christ, we must decide to believe or deny. This entry moment into the theater determines whether we dance or fall off the lip of the stage.

Once that decision is made, everything changes. We discover that the story changes us as we are acting out our parts, and all of this is done in perfect harmony with the Director's desires. We now dance to the beat of a different drum. Heaven's theater is crowded with those who have rejected their past and refused to be defined by the opinions of others.

In the Old Testament there was a Judge in Israel by the name of Jephthah. His mother was a prostitute, and his brothers, who happened to have been born legitimately, kicked him out of the house for the shame he brought them. Talk about a rough start in life, and yet, Jephthah refused to be characterized by those two early blows. He rose to be a mighty Judge of God's people, ultimately delivering them from their enemies. Jephthah never allowed people or circumstances to define him, and neither should we let others hinder our performance. There are also no size restrictions on heaven's stage as a man in the first century discovered.

"Zacchaeus was a wee little man, and a wee little man was he. He climbed up in a sycamore tree for the Lord he wanted to see," as the song goes. Being short of stature, Zacchaeus must have elbowed his way through the crowd to get a look at this miracle working carpenter from Nazareth. Hopping up and down, he, no doubt, looked for a group of children to join to get a good vantage point. Refusing to give up, he climbed a sycamore tree. Zacchaeus waited till Jesus passed by, and when he did, the Master looked up and saw the determined face of the tax collector. His reward was to receive Jesus as a house guest that very day.

However, Zacchaeus had to overcome something more than his height restriction when he hosted Jesus. His occupation caused him to be hated by the people of Jericho. Zacchaeus's only friends were sinners and tax collectors just like himself. It is to be noted that wherever Jesus went, he caused a ruckus. In this case, rather than visiting a dignitary of the city, he choose to be entertained by a house full of societal outcasts. The acceptance and love that Zacchaeus experienced that day changed his life. With the raising of his glass, he promised to repay any he had wronged and give away half of his wealth to the poor.

The words of the critics' sound like a mighty roar in comparison to the quiet encouragement of the Director. Voices from our past haunt us. That horrible thing that happened years ago looms large in our minds. We can rise above both people and circumstances by embracing the invitation of the casting call. Never allow your past to define you. Nevertheless, it is sometimes a great struggle to answer the call to join heaven's stage.

C.S. Lewis, by his own admission, came kicking and thrashing to Christ. Like a rebellious schoolboy, who had finally been corralled, his eyes were "darting in every direction."[59] He had desperately wanted not to be "interfered with."[60] Concerning his battle to believe Lewis writes, "you must picture me alone in that room in Magdalen, night after night, feeling, whenever my mind lifted even for a second from my work, the steady, unrelenting approach of him whom I so desperately desire not to meet. That which I greatly feared had it last come upon me. In the Trinity Term of 1929 I gave in, and admitted that God was God, and knelt and prayed: perhaps, that night, the most dejected and reluctant convert in all England."[61]

Close to the point of believing in God, Lewis examined himself and what he found appalled him; "A zoo of lusts, a bedlam of ambitions, a nursery of fears, a harem of fondled hatreds. His name was Legion."[62] When he finally surrendered to Christ, he joyfully confessed that, "the great Angler played His fish and I never dreamed that the hook was in my tongue."[63] All along Lewis's journey to heaven's theater, the Casting Director had been applying the gentle pressure of a skilled fisherman in landing his catch in the boat. The drawing power of the Holy Spirit is undeniably wonderful.

While serving in the military overseas, I sensed a drawing from the Lord. At first I resisted, but he was relentless. After months of wandering deeper and deeper into the empty cavern of my soul, I finally reach a point of desperation. In the countryside of Italy, by three large bushes, I finally gave my heart to the Director. The skies were bright blue, the clouds large and puffy on the day of my transformation from darkness to light. Another flawed player joined the troupe to tell God's story.

Occasionally, I think back to those who have been in my life even before my entrance onto heaven's stage. Long before that glorious day, in that Italian countryside, his hand had been upon me. I recall the moment I almost fell off a cliff, and my brother's strong hand pushed me back toward the rock wall. There was a summer afternoon that I drove out of a side road and was almost hit by a semi-tractor trailer. These were the times that the Director preserved my life. This guiding hand of the Producer has been called prevenient grace. It is the grace that all men have throughout life, which prepares them to receive Christ. It is the rain that falls on the just and the unjust, and the sun that warms every man's face.[64] The Director places us all onto the stage of life and then graciously watches over us. He guides us to the place where we can choose to be a part of his story.

If you've ever been cast in a play, then you have experienced the first day on a set. Those first few moments, as you are gathered with the rest of the actors and actresses can be awkward. With the weeks and months of rehearsals ahead, you are staring into the faces of sometimes total strangers. We look for connections and we hope for chemistry.

Good acting is not just about spewing out lines with the correct facial expressions. Our need to master timing and develop the smooth dialogue needed to carry the show are bound up in a group of people you know little about. Success on the stage requires seamless interaction with other performers, and that involves interaction with others. Timing and rhythm are crucial between those who share a stage. The ovation at the end is reliant on masterful attention to details within the individual scene. On heaven's stage the Casting Director seems determined to place together the most unlikely characters. This reality leaves us scratching our heads. We have to trust that he knows what he is doing. One of the most important ways that he develops our character is by placing us next to some of the most unusual characters we will ever meet. Think of all the chance encounters we have, and how we are thrust into situations on the job site and in school. The people who cross our path do so by divine appointment.

When you consider the billions of people who live on the planet, and the multitudes who have danced across earth's stage from the very beginning of time, those we share our individual stage with is incredibly small. And yet, each one is vital to our development. The Director has carefully chosen every person you have rubbed shoulders with from our first breath. Our rough edges have been knocked off by those who opposed us, and those same rough edges have been polished by those who have loved us. An individual star adds to a brilliant display when placed carefully in the tapestry of the night sky. None of us are alone and no man is an island.

It is important to quietly reflect and seek to understand the fellow cast members that the Director has given you. It is a good thing to pull out the old movies in your mind and see the important people whom he has brought into our lives. Our immediate family ties were chosen for us long before we entered our life experience. We had nothing to do with selecting our parents or siblings. As the old saying goes, we may choose our friends, but we are stuck with our relatives. Regardless, our families were a vital part of our experience.

Every relationship, no matter how deep or shallow impacted us in our moments on life's stage. From your first friend to your last enemy, the Director makes no mistakes. Each fellow actor has changed us in some way. One of the more interesting classes I had in college was an acting class taught by a woman who had performed on Broadway. In all my academic pursuits, I cannot remember a more diverse class of people. All people groups were represented as well as differing political persuasions and lifestyle variations. Yet, there we all were, interacting with each other. Surprisingly, we had more in common than I thought we would, and we all generally liked each other.

To seek out those only of a kindred spirit hinders us from character development. If the people around us simply rubber stamp all of our ideas, and nod with approval when we present our positions, we cease to grow as human beings. Having our ego stroked by the constant approval of others, only drives us deeper into the bubble of our own small world. We should challenge ourselves in situations and with people that are different and sometimes a bit unusual. The Bible certainly offers us some strange individuals.

For example, John the Baptizer was an unusual man to say the least. He was the kind of fellow who never quite fit into society. You probably wouldn't have invited him to your Bar Mitzvah. Showing up at the door with a plate of honey-covered locust would have earned him a trip back into the wilderness, and yet, he was exactly as God created him. I have a sneaking suspicion that God delights in using curiously odd people. Those that the world rejects, he calls.

The Baptizer's father received a prophecy concerning his son. Zachariah was informed that John would preach in the spirit of Elijah. The fact that John lived in the wilderness and preached thunderous messages perfectly matched that prophecy. Even the Baptizer's appearance resembled the sage of old. Before John was even formed in the womb, his strange lifestyle was predicted by his Creator. The Director saw John's life played out before he drew his first breath and fashioned him perfectly for the part. Every life, no matter the circumstances surrounding it or the shape it takes, is perfectly fitted for heaven's stage. There is not a person who has ever been born that the Director has not called to be a part of his story.

Moses was sure that the Casting Director had made a mistake. After reading the script, given to him through a burning bush, the adopted son of Pharaoh simply turned away and smiled. Perhaps years ago, he would have been qualified for such a calling, but now he was old, and the dust of the desert had clogged his thinking. The bleating of sheep had dulled his hearing. Besides, he could not put a decent sentence together to save his skin. For the last forty years a flock of goats and sheep had been his only audience, and now the Lord was asking him to stand before the most powerful man on earth.

The greatest privilege in this life is to realize that we have all been called to be a part of a story greater than ourselves. The Director is knocking on your dressing room door with your part in hand. He has been grooming you from day one to be an indispensable actor in the "big show."

CHAPTER 5

Quiet on the Set

Alfred Hitchcock was known as a master of suspense and one of the greatest movie directors of all time. Born in England to William and Emma Hitchcock, he directed over fifty films in a span of six decades. His fame grew over the years as he invoked fear and high drama in the hearts of those who went to see his movies. In such films as, *Northwest by Northwest, The Man Who Knew Too Much,* and, of course, *The Birds,* he held audiences *Spellbound.* Interestingly, his passion for horror began at an early age.

When Hitchcock was five years old, his father sent him to a local prison with a note for the jailor. After reading the father's scribblings, the officer locked young Alfred in a cell for five minutes. Upon his release, the copper looked at the lad and said, "this is what we do to naughty boys." His father intended to scare him into a life of right living, but the results were quite different. Hitchcock *was* terrified; however, the experience yielded an unexpected outcome. His time in the cell lit a fire within him that would launch him toward his life's work. In a twisted way, the boy enjoyed being frightened by the restraints of steel bars and a musty, cramped room. He would spend the rest of his life attempting to pass that pleasure on to his audiences.

One of the keys to Hitchcock's success was the use of camera angles and lighting to heighten fear within the viewer. The famous shower scene in *Psycho* and the variety of lighting techniques used in *Rear Window* were just a few examples. Furthermore, his personal involvement in every part of every scene was well known to the actors and actresses who were privileged to have worked with him.

As director, Hitchcock was firmly in charge of all his movies and demanded full control of each scene. When he walked onto the set, all eyes were on the Director and all ears open to his instructions. The command to be, "quiet on the set" held heavy sway in the presence of Alfred Hitchcock. Actors and actresses alike listened carefully to his directions. They hung on his every word because to Hitchcock, getting the scene just right was more important than whatever might roll off the thespian's golden tongue. All mouths closed; all ears open, was the edict on the set of a Hitchcock film.

A.M. Nagler, in his book, *A Source Book In Theatrical History*, records this concerning the director, "Though unable to act himself, he should be able to teach others and be the finger-post, guide, philosopher and friend of every soul in a theater, male or female, from the manager and author to the call-boy and the gasman, from the manageress, and principal soprano to the back row of the extra children's ballet and the cleaners."[65] However, this description, posted in the 19th century, falls flat without the attentive ear of all those who inhabit the stage. Those around the Director must listen. Taking direction from the one in charge, willingly, is not an option.

In the grand scheme of life, listening is always more important than speaking. God gave us two ears positioned on each side of our head and only one mouth placed directly under our nose. We should listen intently to others and sniff carefully when words roll off our own tongues. The stench of the rotten things we might say at any given moment is always a danger in our relationships. The same is true on heaven's stage. "Be not rash with your mouth, nor let your heart be hasty to utter a word before God, for God is in heaven and you are on earth. Therefore, let your words be few."[66] In contrast, the still, small voice of the Director is a precious commodity, and we do well to heed it.

The prophet Elijah learned that lesson while hiding from a wicked queen named Jezebel. In a cave, alone and afraid, the wooly-haired preacher was cowering in a hillside crevice. All this, after he faced-off against Jezebel's minions on Mount Caramel. Apparently, he could stand before a horde of false preachers but was terrified of King Ahab's evil wife. Oh, the scourge of an angry woman!

After voicing his complaint to the Lord from the confines of the dark cave, Elijah was told to stand on the mount. A rushing wind passed by followed by a violent earthquake, and then a hot blast of fire, but God's voice was not heard in those loud commotions. Instead, he spoke to his Prophet with a still, small voice. He does the same for us today. Sadly, the roar of life can drown out his cues, and, if we are waiting for a trumpet blast, we will discover God rarely works that way. The rhythm of nature itself is slow and steady, producing seasons without announcement and change without fanfare. God is constantly at work. We must train our ears to listen.

In our brief dance across life's stage, there are critical moments when the Director's voice is heard in the shadows, whispering softly, "Quiet on the set!" He steps down from his chair and waves for all movement to cease. At that point, our listening ear and open heart are paramount. We may be deeply involved in our busy lives, but all distractions must grind to a halt lest we miss his prompt. The divine interruption may seem ill-timed, but unless we listen intently to the Director, our part in his story may be missed. He speaks with a still, small voice, and he does so in a myriad of ways. Whether through circumstances, family or friends, or even enemies, he speaks. He doesn't mince words; he is extremely clear. Without exception, everyone has those pivotal moments in their lives, even the mighty.

Nebuchadnezzar was one of the most powerful rulers of all time. His accomplishments were amazing. He enriched Babylon, one of the greatest cities the world has ever known, and he was admired and feared by the ancient world. He built hanging gardens so that his wife would not be homesick from the land of her origin. The temples he erected in the city were magnificent, along with wall fortifications to protect the people. A deep moat also surrounded the city giving added safety to those who called Babylon home. His use of one of the most precious metals on earth, caused Babylon to be known as the city of gold.

However, Nebuchadnezzar made a fundamental mistake. He became consumed by his own success on his own tiny stage. He took top billing when the real tribute should have gone to the King of heaven. Filled with pride, he lifted his voice and claimed credit for his achievements, "At the end of twelve months he was walking on the roof of the royal palace of Babylon, and the king answered and said, 'Is not this great Babylon, which I have built by my mighty power as a royal residence and for the glory of my majesty?'"[67] While the words were in his mouth God struck him down.

Solomon wrote that pride comes before a fall and nowhere is that truth more evident than in Nebuchadnezzar's pompous parade of prideful arrogance. The King experienced a debilitating crash from atop his palace, driving him out into the field to eat grass like an animal. Simply put, God took his sanity away. For three and a half years his nails grew long, and his beard became shaggy. When the Director calls for quiet on the set, he certainly has some unique ways to get our attention. He stops us in our tracks.

The Lord speaks to the heart of man, and we do well to listen. The rush of life may swirl around us, but his hand in that moment is unmistakable. He presses down upon us until his Spirit encircles us with an unmistakable presence. These moments are really quite indescribable. As the old Scots would say, "It's better felt than telt."

In these surreal moments, we must choose our path forward carefully. Refusing to yield the stage to the One who owns the theatre brings calamity. We may be on top of the world or in the lowest valley, but regardless, to rebuff his divine interruption is to court our own demise. In contrast, to accept his call brings delight and relief.

To enter heaven's stage is not accomplished through an audition. The King of Babylon was given back his sanity when he acknowledged the true King of heaven. It is by a heart surrendered and yielded to Christ that we walk through those theater doors. Before Nebuchadnezzar lost his mind, he had accomplished much in the eyes of men, but in heaven, he was a box office disaster. Let a man make a great name for himself in this world, and he will be forgotten before his dead body grows cold. Nothing occurs of eternal value until the great Director steps in and takes control of our lives. This includes the great and small moments.

Fortunately for Nebuchadnezzar, he made the right decision. He declared, "At the end of the days I, Nebuchadnezzar, lifted my eyes to heaven, and my reason returned to me, and I blessed the Most High, and praised and honored him who lives forever, for his dominion is an everlasting dominion, and his kingdom endures from generation to generation; all the inhabitants of the earth are accounted as nothing, and he does according to his will among the host of heaven and among the inhabitants of the earth; and none can stay his hand or say to him, "What have you done?"[68] It certainly sounds like Nebuchadnezzar entered God's redemptive story and eventually entered the real City of Gold.

When the Author of life enters our emptiness, all idols come crashing down, and we are swept into his story. We suddenly realize that the only true foundation of life is found in Jesus. Embraced by a love we cannot explain we become speechless. We are captured by the Director in a wonderful trap designed for our freedom. Such was the case in the life of one of the early disciples.

There was a young and ambitious Jew who lived during the first century whose name was Saul. He discovered, in a most unusual way, that running from the One who was calling him to heaven's stage was futile. It all began on the road to Damascus as Saul led a search party to imprison the followers of Jesus. It is a story of the pursuer, becoming the pursued; of the hunter becoming the hunted...

The noonday sun beat down on the young Pharisee as he approached the city. List in hand, he had been granted the authority to hunt down every man and woman whose names appeared on the parchment. Like a ravenous wolf, Saul hid in the shelter of his beloved religion, Judaism, and ruthlessly craved his pound of flesh from the disciples of Jesus. Undeterred by conscience, he killed and imprisoned those who had chosen heaven's stage. He should have known better, but alas, he was blinded by pride and driven by ambition.

Stepping back, Saul was a remarkable man. Steeped in intellect and grounded in a monotheistic religion, wherein the God of Israel was worshiped by carefully subscribed sacrifices, he excelled. His family's pedigree was deep and impressive. His climb to the top of the religious ladder was a foregone conclusion. Admired by friends and family alike, the quest to sit on the council of the Sanhedrin would be another impressive achievement, another notch on his belt. However, deep down within Saul, there was a tug, an annoying sense of dread which disturbed his peace and ruined the delight he should have been experiencing in his pursuit of religious perfection. It was as if a cattle prod was poking him in the side, forcing him down a strange, new path.

Cresting the hill, he saw Damascus ahead. The city appeared as a white diamond against the desert sand. Like an animal approaching its prey, Saul slowed his pace. His eyes scanned the city. After checking his list, he continued walking. Placing his hand upon his donkey he scratched her rough hide and smiled. Through the last few months, she had been his closest ally, perhaps his only friend. Once this nasty business of rounding up these Nazarenes was finished, he would reward her with a grassy field.

Suddenly, something unexpected happened, something that changed his life. A light, brighter than the noon-day sun, struck him to the ground. Blinded by the piercing rays, he scratched in the desert sand, searching for his precious list. Reaching out for his bellowing donkey, he suddenly felt a blow to his side. Her kicking hoofs had found its mark. Fearing she had cracked his ribs; he fought to get away. Sand pummeled his face. The sound of his trusty sidekick grew faint as she ran off into the distance. The men who were with him ran for cover. Crippled and confused, Saul, who had moments before been plotting the demise of others, now lay in the hot desert sand. Attempting to get up, he heard a voice that was calm and steady. It carried a hint of sadness. The voice asked a question that Saul himself had been wrestling with for weeks.

"Saul, Saul why do you persecute me? It is hard to resist that which persistently goads you in a certain direction."[69]

The proud Pharisee thought back to the preceding months. The eyes of those he had imprisoned came flooding into his mind. Some had been fearful while others looked into his eyes with love and compassion. These rebels were attempting to destroy the religion that he loved, or so he thought. They deserved what they got, and yet, he could not escape his own guilt. Steven's stoning haunted him. The man had died with a blaze of glory on his face. Saul had never witnessed anything like it. What was it about these people that caused them to stand firmly in the face of death and imprisonment? If he was doing God's work, why was he so guilt ridden?

Saul, whose tongue was normally freewheeling, now struggled to ask the question that would change his life. He knew who it was that spoke to him, and yet, he asked. His words tumbled out, filled with fear and trepidation.

"Who are you, sir?" The answer changed his life. It was Jesus of Nazareth.

Saul was on the fast track to the top of the Jewish religion until he was abruptly interrupted on the road to Damascus. Jesus stopped him dead in his tracks. His pedigree and training dissolved instantly on that dusty trail. He who attempted to squash the good news of Jesus like a bug became its greatest proponent.

Looking back, Saul was an interesting choice. A Roman citizen by birth, he had spent his early years in Tarsus, a town known for its Greek culture and learning. While still a lad, he had been sent to be tutored under the watchful eye of Gamaliel the Elder, the great Rabbi of Israel. Interestingly, his angry hunt for the followers of Christ did not stop him from being cast by the Director. Wandering into Damascus, he was led by the hand of a friend to the home of a Jesus follower. Saul had to become blind before he could finally see. He discovered that if the Lord could rescue him, he could rescue anyone.

It is futile to run and hide backstage or sneak into the dressing room when God calls our name. The One who holds the script insists on a decision, and nothing less will satisfy him. To answer no, or put off the choice, casts a shadow over the rest of life. Rejection bears a cost that must be eventually paid, and we instinctively know it. When that time comes, and there may be several of them, the decision we make affects all of our eternity. As for Saul, the rest is history. Arriving in Damascus he found shelter with the very people he had planned to hunt down. A man named Ananias, who had been packing to get out of town, prayed for Paul to receive his sight. Ananias then embraced the man he had previously feared. The rebel would become the Apostle to the Gentiles as his shackles were removed from his eyes. His own narrative had to be abandoned so that he could step onto heaven's stage. His tongue had to be stilled so he could begin to use it for a higher audience. The Director cried, "Quiet on the set," and Saul of Tarsus became Paul the Apostle.

All of life before that moment has prepared us to listen carefully to our calling to submit to Jesus Christ as Lord and Savior. Long before we walked into love's snare, the Playwright was busy arranging all the details. He even works from generation to generation to build his acting troupe as in the case of a lonely Bible teacher in Massachusetts.

Edward Kimball was a Sunday School teacher in Boston during the mid 1850s. He had a burden for the boys who attended his weekly Bible class. One in particular was Dwight Moody. Moody worked in his uncle's shop, the Holton Shoe Store, as a boot salesman. One day Kimball visited young Dwight at his place of business. Pacing back and forth in front of the store, Kimball finally decided to enter and press upon Moody his need for Christ. That day, in the back storage room, the young man was converted.

Dwight Moody preached for many years, reaching thousands for Christ. One of the men converted under his ministry was Wilbur Chapman. Chapman became an evangelist, traveling far and wide, spreading the good news of the gospel. As a result of his preaching, a young man named Billy Sunday came to Christ. The former baseball professional left the diamond and entered the pulpit. Under his ministry, a man named Mordecai Ham joined God's theater and became a preacher. Mordecai Ham visited North Carolina, and in one of his revival services, a young gentleman came forth by the name of Billy Graham to claim Christ as his Savior.

This amazing chain of events could only have been arranged by the Playwright. There is an old saying, "you can count the apples on the tree, but who can count the apples in a seed." Edward Kimball overcame a case of nerves to plant a seed that changed the landscape of God's theater. In the back room of that lowly shoe store, God was at work to fill his stage. Imagine Kimball's delight when heaven's theater throws its final cast party.

In our journey to the main stage, it is the Director who pulls back the curtain and prepares our entrance. We make the decision, but he is still fully in charge. "We love because he first loved us."[70] In his book, *The Pursuit of God*, A.W. Tozer surprised me. What I expected to be a treatise on man's search for God turned out to be something quite the opposite.

Tozer's thesis was God's unrelenting pursuit of man. He writes, "We pursue God because, and only because, he has first put an urge within us that spurs us to the pursuit. "No man can come to me," said our Lord, "except the Father which hath sent me draw him." The impulse to pursue God originates with God, but the outworking of that impulse is our hard following after him, and all the time we are pursuing him, we are already in his hand: "Thy right hand upholds me."[71] The Director's passion for our soul knows no bounds.

The importance of our decision to be quiet on the set cannot be overstated. The fact that each man's story is being played out on earth does not negate his responsibility to see beyond this life into eternity. This life is only Act One of an eternal drama that reaches its dynamic climax in our response to his invitation. It is possible to dance and sing with such fury that we fall off the stage into an eternity without God. It is possible to blast our own horn so loudly that it is the only song we hear. We can miss the entire purpose for our existence by following lesser paths, or by accepting inferior roles. We must be humble enough to face the fact of our great need for Jesus. Reaching out to him with the faith of a child is the only way onto heaven's stage. Denying him dooms our temporary performance, landing us in a place of eternal destruction.

As Jesus passed through the dusty little towns of Israel, the children who wandered across his path were no doubt a delight to him. Their simple and sincere trust drew him to them. No pretense or guile was found in their hearts, for they just wanted to be loved. I can picture Jesus gathering under the shade of a fig tree with a dozen youngsters and enjoying every minute. Their eyes were wide, their hearts were open, and it thrilled the Master's soul to teach them. They were not bogged down with life's concerns, neither were they scrambling to develop some sort of philosophy to replace their simple faith. Their chalkboards were free from the scribbling of human foolishness, and their minds were not muddled with self-loathing concerns. They had no difficulty receiving his love or his teaching. Little wonder he told his followers that they must become like children before they could enter the Kingdom of heaven. "Quiet on the set," reaches the heart of the uncluttered soul.

Furthermore, it is by the mercy of the Playwright that he stirs us out of our lethargy. The wellspring of humility recognizes this truth, "No one understands; no one seeks for God. All have turned aside; together they have become worthless; no one does good, not even one."[72] We do not seek to be cast in his story any more than a mouse hunts a cat. The hound of heaven pursues the weary fox until slyboots lie exhausted in the bush. The great angler of heaven knows how to set his hook and play his fish. To sit silently and contemplate eternity is not in our nature. Apart from his drawing, we never breach the threshold of our need for him.

To be cognizant of a light that fully reveals our every thought and motive is mind-numbing. And yet, realizing that same light also brings us to the end of ourselves is threatening. His probing Spirit sends us flying into the orchestra pit without an instrument to play. Being pulled out into the open, both hurts and heals us, all at the same time. Being exposed is unsettling. Regardless, it is his relentless love that holds us on the ropes.

Even though God is at work drawing us, it is still our responsibility to respond and that begins with a closed mouth. "Now we know that whatever the law says it speaks to those who are under the law, so that every mouth may be stopped, and the whole world may be held accountable to God."[73] "In the end that Face which is the delight, or the terror of the universe must be turned upon each of us either with one expression or with the other, either conferring glory inexpressible or inflicting shame that can never be cured or disguised."[74]

When we are knocked down on the stage of life, we tend to be more receptive to the Director's voice. His left jabs are landed in just the right places to bring us to our knees. Until we become crippled by the realization of our sin, we cannot hear him speak. The way of the transgressor is hard, and it is supposed to be that way. All the bumps and bruises of life are meant to wear us down and bring us to a place where we will listen to the Director. The emptiness within us calls out. It is in that great moment that we can decide to follow him or continue to go on our own way.

The redeeming love of the Playwright is the theme of life. It is the taproot of the tree from which all of life draws its source. Salvation is the singular element which answers the great questions of humanity and satisfies our longing for all to be made whole again. Every struggle he has sent our way becomes, in that moment, a blessed gift from above. He calls from heaven with a still, small voice that trumpets freedom and forgiveness. He simply asks us to be still and then answer his call.

To those who have entered its mystery, redemption is a fountain of life. His song of redeeming love will be sung throughout eternity. Moreover, the script is filled with stories of God's triumph in the lives of those who chose to follow him. His mighty acts of victory over his sin and death, fill the scenes and dominates the storyline. The libraries of the world cannot hope to chronicle what redemption has penned. In heaven, the ink continues to flow, and the writing paper is abundant. Every detail is written down in grand fashion by heavenly scribes. Every single victory is recorded to be read for all eternity. The stories this world has ignored fill the literary landscape in heaven, and they all begin with a quiet moment, in a secluded place, listening to a still, small voice.

CHAPTER 6

Break a Leg

It was the Australian novelist, Thomas Michael Keneally, who first introduced us to the amazing life of Oskar Schindler. In his book, *Schindler's Ark*, Keneally recounts the true story of an Austrian businessman who became an unlikely hero. Amazingly, what had begun as a plan to fill his factory with workers became so much more by the end of World War II. At some point, within the darkest days of human history, the aspiring entrepreneur emerged as the means God used to rescue over a thousand Jews from certain death.

As his purpose shifted from cheap labor to saving lives, the German industrialist and member of the Nazi party became a hero to the Jewish nation. It began with a dawning realization of an injustice so great as to shake Schindler's world. In his book, Keneally notes, "To write these things now is to state the common places of history. But to find them out in 1942, to have them break upon you from a June sky, was to suffer a fundamental shock, a derangement in that area of the brain in which the stable ideas of humankind and its possibilities are kept."[75]

Schindler's "fundamental shock," altered the direction of his life. By the time the war was over he would lose everything in exchange for a priceless legacy. He became penniless, and at the same time, wealthy beyond imagination. Through unexpected detours, brought to bear by harsh realities, Schindler left behind a legacy of sacrificial service to his fellow man. So, how did it all begin?

The story began when Schindler hired a Jewish woman named Itzhak Stern to keep his accounts. With a burdened heart for her people, Stern encouraged him to hire Jews bound for concentration camps. Even though many of them possessed little skill for the work, Schindler saw an opportunity for cheap labor. However, as the atrocities of the Nazi regime increased, his vision changed. Selfish motives changed to selfless sacrifice as he began to use his resources to bribe Nazi officers in exchange for more Jewish workers to his factory. In doing so he placed himself in great danger.

As the smoke of the great European conflict settled, and uncertainty loomed over most of the continent, Schindler's deeds were being celebrated on heaven's stage. Oskar Schindler gained the gratitude of the Jewish nation as generations of Jews are alive today because of him. The atrocities of World War II, witnessed by Schindler, wounded his heart and changed the direction of his life. On heaven's stage what happened to Schindler is a common experience. It is the wounds of life that propel us onto greater things and new purposes. It is the experiences we would have never chosen that give us a life we never could have imagined. In effect, God must injure us to heal us from ourselves.

When an actor or actress is told to *break a leg*, it is an encouragement to give all they have to the performance. However, even though the phrase is commonly used, no one knows it's origin. Some say it goes back to the ancient Greeks, where, instead of applauding, a grateful audience would stomp their feet. If they pounded the floor hard enough, they would break a leg. It is doubtful that this literally happened, but it is an interesting theory. Fast forward to the Elizabethan Age and the practice of rewarding a good performance was displayed with the banging of chairs on the floor. The possibility of one of those chairs breaking a leg was evidence of a great show. Again, just speculation.

The modern theory points to a line toward the back of the stage called a "leg line." Behind that line stood those who were waiting to be called onto the stage. To break the *leg line* meant that you stepped over the line and entered the performance. In the end, the term is wrapped in a riddle and buried in an enigma. Perhaps, in the great drama of eternal events on earth, the term can bring a new meaning altogether. Howbeit, I would like to borrow the phrase and give it a new meaning.

Rather than encouraging a great performance, perhaps the phrase, "break a leg," could be used in a different way. To break a leg is the moment in the story that appears to cripple the main character in a metaphorical sense. The injury may be physical, psychological, or it might damage the human spirit, but whatever the wound, it is both permanent and debilitating. The moment calls out to the will of the main character to decide the direction of the play. It is such a dramatic occurrence that the character never fully recovers.

At that point in the production, roles surrounding the lead actor must be redefined according to the hero's decision to either give up or find the courage to press on. The story takes on new meaning as the following question looms large before the audience. Will the one who has received the deafening blow recover to go on to greater deeds, or will he or she succumb to despair and exit life's struggle? The difference determines whether the play will be a comedy or a tragedy, providing either a happy ending or a tragic conclusion.

In Victor Hugo's masterpiece, *Les Misérables*, a handsome young woodcutter named Jean Valjean is cruelly sentenced to prison for stealing a loaf of bread to feed his hungry family. He is released only to be pursued by the heartless inspector, Javert. Settling in a new town under a different name, Valjean longs for the shadow of his shame to be lifted, and his true identity never to be discovered. Will he be returned to prison, or will he overcome his past by living a virtuous life under a different identity? This story draws us in because its theme is true to life. We have all been jousted with consequences that deeply changed us. We have all run from shame and tried to start anew.

In theater, where the unexpected is commonplace, and the winds of chance dance on the head of a pin, the story dies an early death without crisis. Hamstringing the lead with impending calamity plunges the drama to deeper levels and benefits the overall performance. The devious villain with his evil scheme excites us. When catastrophe enters the narrative, the story is elevated to new heights, creating tension and anxiety. The focus of the audience is riveted on the characters as blood pressure rises. If this axiom is true in theater, why should it not be in life?

However, break a leg moments aren't only for the main actor. Those whose time on the stage is short lived, who are in a supporting role, enhance the overall production when wounds occur.

Dillion Wells was all of 19 years old when the Playwright wrote into his story a plot twist that no one saw coming. Rising from his bed on the morning of July 12th, 2012, he took three steps and collapsed on the floor never to walk again. Struck down by a disease that afflicts one in a million, family and friends struggled to come to terms with Dillion's prognosis.

However, life was not over for this young man as he refused to be defined by his new path. Rather than surrender to self-pity and discouragement, Dillion persistently followed his dreams. He earned his college degree, worked at a major theme park, and became engaged to a lovely young lady named Catherine. Through an apparent tragedy came the light of a full life. He lived unfettered until the day he died.

Friends and family packed his funeral service to express what his life meant to them. Even the Dignity website, that housed comments about his life, crashed because of the volume of entries. His life, cut short in the eyes of the world, was a full performance in the eyes of the Director. Even as the curtain fell, his story continues to be told in the lives he left behind.

The events that appear to cripple us are gifts from the Scripter. The blows of life direct us to detours leading to new adventures. We have impact in the lives of others when we have been impacted ourselves. We gain an audience in our afflictions. Those who have been broken by life tend to produce the most important lines and moments on stage. A.W. Tozer wrote, "It is doubtful God can use anyone greatly until He has hurt him deeply."[76]

Tozer's quote may seem difficult for some, but when we analyze it, his words begin to make perfect sense. None of us are born with great character. Nobility in spirit is best forged in the furnace of difficulty. The gold that rises to the surface only does so in extreme heat. There is far too much dross in all of us that needs to be removed.

This leads us to the perplexing dilemma of why God allows pain and suffering. It is a simple inquiry that ought to have a simple answer, but it has so mystified the minds of men that no amount of writing in any book, nor debate, has truly answered the question. Unfortunately, the solutions that *are* offered become more problematic than the question itself.

Wise men all the way back to the time of Job have wrestled with this dark conundrum. Job's friends offered this judgmental observation, "Remember: who that was innocent ever perished? Or where were the upright cut off? As I have seen, those who plow iniquity and sow trouble reap the same. By the breath of God, they perish, and by the blast of his anger they are consumed." As the old saying goes, "With friends like that, who needs enemies."

By faith we declare that God is good, and yet, bones break, and hearts disintegrate in the blast of life's furnace. The Playwright allows evil to flourish and tolerates wickedness to persist. He did send fire down on Sodom, and he did judge the Egyptians for the treatment of his people, but those are the exceptions. His practice seems to be this: he allows evil to continue and then somehow uses it for his ends. Still, our minds reject such notions. If Aristotle's definition of a good life is happiness, then pain and suffering strip us of that potential.

In regard to Job, the world was his oyster. All the planets aligned at his birth as the cosmos seemed to say, 'This fellow gonna have a perfect life.' Like Curly McLain in Oklahoma, he sang out as the sun rose, "oh what a beautiful morning, oh what a beautiful day, I've got a beautiful feelin' everything's goin' my way." Like cornstalks that grew clear up to the sky, Job had seven sons and three daughters. His business was as successful as a blossoming prairie ranch on the Oklahoma plain. He was a wealthy man, and yet, he refused to allow his riches to go to his head. Admired by the men of his time, it seemed like nothing could disturb his harmonious bliss. However, all of that changed in a single day. His downhill spiral was unforeseen and shocking to say the least. It was a plot twist to end all plot twists, and it was initiated by the Scriptwriter.

The story begins with a quaint family tradition. His sons and daughters, now grown, had gathered at the eldest son's home to have a birthday party. Little did they know that this would be their last day on earth. Disaster struck as four messengers of doom, each on the heels of the other, delivered to Job and his wife the worst news anyone could receive. On a given day his livestock was stolen, his sheep and servants were reduced to ashes by lightning strikes, a group of marauding Chaldeans had raided his camels, and then to finish the worst single day any man had ever endured, all his children died as the timbers of their house came crashing down upon them. Even those who see the glass half-full would turn the cup upside down. In fact, the only person left after the dust settled was the perennial pessimist, Job's wife. Let's rewind.

Job was a good father. He and his wife were enjoying being empty nesters. They were cruising toward their golden years. Nothing but happy, sunny days ahead. Job thought he had reached his crescendo, his magnum opus, but according to the Playwright he had not even begun the rising action of his life. God decided to flip Job's story with an ending that no one saw coming. A rapid-fire series of events completely changed his landscape and redefined his relationships. God did more than muddy the drinking water, he sent an Oklahoman twister.

Oswald Chambers said, "If we are going to be used by God, He will take us through a multitude of experiences that are not meant for us at all but meant to make us useful in His hands. There are things we go through which are unexplainable on any other line, and the nearer we get to God the more inexplicable the way seems. It is only on looking back and getting an explanation from God's word that we understand His dealings with us."[77]

Dr. William Crawford Gorgas's entire life was affected by the yellow fever that plagued the world over 100 years ago. Fortunately, he did not allow it to define his life. His parents met in Mobile, Alabama in 1853, as a result of a yellow-fever outbreak. William was the first of six children and attending his birth was Alabama's pioneer yellow fever specialist, Dr. Joshua Nott.

Gorgas's desire to join the military led him to become a doctor, and as a young officer in the Army Medical Corps, he was sent to assist in a yellow-fever outbreak in Texas in 1882. During his time there, he attended to a Miss Marie Doughty, the sister-in-law to the post commander. Being critically ill, she was given little hope of surviving the disease. In fact, her grave was already dug, and Gorgas had volunteered to go with the body and read the last rites. But then, the unexpected happened. Gorgas also became sick with yellow fever.

In his book, *The Path between the Seas*," David McCullough writes concerning Gorgas, "But then he too fell ill, nearly died, but recovered, as did Miss Doughty, with the result that they were convalescent at the same time and fell in love. She became the doctor's wife following a visit to Tuscaloosa to meet his widowed mother, and since they were now permanently immune to yellow fever, he would be summoned repeatedly for special duty wherever the disease broke out."[78]

Gorgas eventually became a pioneer in the research that led to the discovery of the source of yellow fever. His work in Havana, Cuba led to millions of lives being saved from the dreaded disease caused by a particular type of mosquito, *Stegomyia fasciata*. Eventually, his work led him to Panama where his efforts helped stem the tide of yellow fever and allow the Panama Canal to be completed. Shrouded by a dreaded disease, Dr. Gorgas's life was used by the Playwright to bring forth relief and hope to multitudes.

However, there is also a spiritual lesson to learn. The 'yellow fever' of bitterness toward God, brought on by suffering, is only cured when we are inoculated with a clear biblical declaration. The Bible states without apology that God is love. Human rationale rejects such a bold assessment, given the world's situation. Yet, what the thinking man rejects as repulsive, the person of faith embraces. Mankind comes to conclusions based on his limited scope of vision while God declares truth grounded in eternity. We will never fully understand why we suffer, but trusting the love of God somehow short-circuits our need to know. We rest in hope, knowing that all things work together for good and for God's purposes.[79]

Also, throughout the centuries, men and women who loved God have been afflicted with pain. Sorrow has plunged them into darkness, giving them insights that are passed on to us. When we are in the midst of pain we look for others who have gone down the same path. Paul offers this insight, "Blessed be the God and Father of our Lord Jesus Christ, the Father of mercies and God of all comfort, who comforts us in all our affliction, so that we may be able to comfort those who are in any affliction, with the comfort with which we ourselves are comforted by God."[80] Books have also been written out of the quagmire of deep grief. *The Problem of Pain*, by C.S. Lewis and *Where Is God When It Hurts*, by Philip Yancey are just a few examples. These books, and others like them, have offered comfort to multitudes.

In God's grand production, no event or circumstance is without purpose. Seemingly tragic moments are full of meaning as God works his manuscript into our lives. In every blow of life, we are sharpened for a higher purpose. Mistakes, big and small, provide the needed clay in the hands of the Potter. They become the cue cards of the Playwright. When unforeseen pain crashes in and threatens to derail our performance, the Director steps in and uses it as a plot twist that brings color to the ongoing scenes of our lives. Compassion for our fellow actors is born through the pressing pain of life. Humility is a by-product of suffering and heartache. Low tides in our lives reveal messages in bottles previously buried in the sand. In this theater called life, the crippling moment is applauded by the heavenly audience because they know their God is at work. As he allows the freewill of man to play out, the Playwright is still firmly in control.

One of the teachings of Jesus involved a pearl of great price. A merchant, upon discovering this beautiful gem of the sea, sold everything he had to purchase it. The merchant understood the pearl's value and was willing to give up all that he possessed to obtain it. What some men would have bartered for, he gladly paid full price, emptying out his bank account to purchase it. Before we look at the application of this story concerning the pearl, it is important to consider what the oyster goes through to produce its prized gem.

It is a parasite that invades the unsuspecting mollusk and begins the process of creating a pearl. The oyster, rather than pushing the intruder away, begins to encase the unwanted guest with the same element it uses to produce its shell. The oyster entraps the parasite forever, and thus, the pearl is formed. In the middle of that beautiful pearl, is an entombed parasite. The intruder which attacks and irritates the oyster, in the end, produces its most valued treasure.

The events of our lives that bring us pain are used by the Director to create beauty. They mold us into something useful and lovely on his stage. This is a great mystery which will only be fully understood in heaven.

Rachel was born with an umbilical cord wrapped around her neck which was only the beginning of her troubles. Her life story was a series of painful memories and damaging relationships, as she played the part of the abused and the abuser. However, Rachel now lives a much different life. She dances and sings to the Director with a heart that is free from its past. She is not a victim; she is an overcomer. Rachel has discovered the secret of joy from the only One who can provide peace from the troubled storms of her life. I count it a great privilege to call her my friend. The following are her own words, as she has given me permission to share.

"There was a very dark time in my childhood when I lived in Europe with my real father and his second wife. It is hard for me to write about it because every time I do my heart breaks for that little girl. For four years I was locked in a room away from the world. I could go to school but as soon as I got home, I was back in that room. I had my own cooking utensils and silverware that I kept in my room. I was let out to cook my meals, take a shower, and to go to the bathroom three times a day. I had to wash my own clothes in a tub and hang them out to dry on the line. I was about nine when this began, and it lasted four years. I did things in those years just to survive. There wasn't always lunch money so I would get a bathroom pass after lunch and go to the outside dumpster to pick through the leftovers from the other kid's lunches. I was also physically and sexually abused by my own father during this time. My stepmother would periodically beat me. I was banished from the family because I refused to say I love you to my stepmother.

I was devastated. I felt unclean, as if I were some kind of monster. I felt like I had done something so horribly wrong that nobody would ever love me. I truly felt broken and shattered. I remember catching flies and tearing their wings off so I could put them in my doll house and talk to them. They were my only companionship during those cruel years. The flies didn't run away from me or abuse me. I know it was a cruel thing to do but at the time I didn't really think of it as hurting them. I was just keeping them with me so I could have friends. Even though they were tiny and didn't talk back to me, they were still my friends.

Yes, it was a very dark time, possibly the darkest time in my life, but while all this was happening, I prayed. I didn't grow up in Christianity, so I only knew bits and pieces about God and Jesus, but I still prayed. I knew that God was with me, and that he surrounded me with angels because I should have gone insane with what I went through. I should have died many times, but God was always there, and I will eternally be grateful for his love and mercy. You might ask how I can have such faith in a loving God with all I have been through. I can truly look back at every day of my life, and amid my suffering, he comforted me. He gave me the strength and peace to carry on.

He has shown me how to love another human being and that I am not a monster. I am not worthless. My life has been a huge struggle, and I still face issues today, but God is with me during my chaos and in my darkest moments. There is a lot more to my story than just what happened in that room. But that time in my life encompasses a myriad of darkness, sadness, brokenness, and pain more than in any other time in my life. God brought me through it, and he will continue to bring me through all the obstacles in my life. We will all face struggles, but, in the pain and strife, God is there. Let Jesus walk with you and let the healing begin." Rachel's life defies logic which is exactly the point. God makes beauty out of ashes.

Stephen, the first martyr of the church, was a shooting star. From serving tables, he was called to be among the first deacons in a fellowship that was growing in leaps and bounds. His boldness in preaching the gospel so infuriated the unbelieving Jews of his day that it earned him a roll down a hill and a flurry of stones. Being pelted with rocks, Stephen looked up into the sky and saw Jesus standing next to the Father welcoming his obedient servant into heaven. His performance earned him one of the grandest standing ovations ever given. It is even more amazing when we consider that Jesus, who sat down next to his Father after he returned to heaven, was now standing. The Director rarely stands, but, in Stephen's case, he made an exception.

This horrific scene was not the only *break a leg* moment that occurred on the day Stephen died. There was another man who stood by, and not only witnessed the deacon's martyrdom, but also orchestrated it. A young man named Saul was holding the garments for the men who committed the heinous crime that day. Watching Stephen die, Saul's rugged resistance received a crack in its foundation. He had never seen a man so full of glory amid such a brutal attack of hatred. Like a hole in the dike, a trickle of water appeared. Before long, the pressure of Stephen's one grand stage performance was too much for Saul to bear. The dam was about to break.

The Director used the death of Stephen to call onto the stage one of the greatest actors his theatre has ever known. This was Saul's recollection of the moment as he stood before a crowd of hostile men years later, "And when the blood of Stephen your witness was being shed, I myself was standing by and approving and watching over the garments of those who killed him."[81] Saul was drawn to heaven's theater and to the Director he once hated because of Steven's faithful performance.

We all desire a long and productive career on life's stage, but that is not always the will of the Playwright. A long life is not always a full life. Stephen's death was Saul's *break a leg* moment. Saul, now Paul the apostle, launched out in a new direction. His long ministry building churches was made possible by Steven's brief dance across life's stage. It is the Director who decides our life's purpose and longevity.

An honest evaluation of our lives reveals we have very little control over the script. We did not choose the day of our birth, neither will we choose the time of our death. The color of our eyes and hair as well as our body type was thrust upon us at birth with no consideration of our input. We didn't go shopping for our parents nor siblings. Whether we were born with a silver spoon in our mouth or a rusty fork in our ear didn't come up for a vote. We simply opened our eyes, and the spotlight of life hit us square in the face.

The question is not if we will suffer, but how much and in what way. Life leaves none of us without scars. Our *break a leg* moment advances his story in some mysterious ways. "In theater, every stumble is an opportunity to dance."[82] Remember, light shines through cracked pots.

None of us like life-altering times, but in the Playwright's script, they all serve a purpose. To the question of pain, no answer fully satisfies in this lifetime. The best we can do is carefully collect some comforting thoughts until we stand before the Director in that glorious day. And so, with that disclaimer in place, we proceed in life on the premise that some elements of our story must wait until the final curtain call. The severe tragedies and deep heartaches of this life will be fully redeemed when our stories move to heaven. The spotlight can be hot and blinding causing us to wonder if we are deserted on the stage, but we are not alone; we have never been alone. It is not until we walk into eternity that we will realize that the Playwright does all things well.

Our lives are not finished until God says so, and he is working all things for our good and his glory regardless of our perspective. There is purpose even in our darkest times. Peter's sorrow, after his denial, was replaced with the joy of a personal visit with the resurrected Christ. The woman with the issue of blood was suddenly healed by Jesus, offering a powerful testimony to those who were listening to the Master. The pain Jairus experienced at the death of his daughter was replaced by joy when Jesus raised her back to life. The three apostles, who were in the inner circle, were deeply impacted by that moment. The Scriptwriter knows what he is doing, and our opera is not over until the fat lady sings.

Sin entered humanity like a parasite at the beginning, bringing with it pain and suffering. God has chosen not to insulate us from its fiery blast. In his infinite wisdom, he has decided to use it for his purposes. The sculptor's tools cut and shave until the masterpiece is revealed. It is not a pretty process, but the Playwright allows it to further his Kingdom.

Consider again the oyster. If the parasite never enters its shell the oyster could live out its life unperturbed. Dying of old age or being eaten by a hungry sea star would have been its lot in life. No value beyond itself would have been gained other than a meal for a blue crab. However, with the introduction of the parasite, the hard-shelled crustacean protects itself by surrounding the irritant with a calcium deposit which eventually becomes a pearl. It now offers the land above the saltwater marsh something of lasting value.

In the end, pain and suffering will be eradicated. The parasite of sin will be gone forever. His followers are the pearl of great price that Jesus died to redeem. The pearl, that suffering produces, reaches its ultimate expression of beauty when it adorns the One who purchased it. When we walk into the new Jerusalem, we will be entering through gates created of singular pearls. "And the twelve gates were twelve pearls, each of the gates made of a single pearl, and the street of the city was pure gold, like transparent glass."[83] Those twelve pearls will be drilled out, leaving the centers gone forever. The parasite that helped form the pearl will be banished from memory. Our wounds will be healed forever in that heavenly city. Jesus promised that he is making all things new, but *how* new is impossible to presently comprehend. All shame will be gone, and every tear will be wiped away. Oh, the glory of our eternal home. We will be free at last from the weight of this life and the pain we have suffered.

CHAPTER 7

Rags to Riches

Rags to riches stories in the world of both theater and literature are common fare. In Dickens's classic, *Oliver Twist*, young Oliver goes from asking, "more soup please," to becoming modestly wealthy. Albeit, in the interim, the boy, who was abandoned at birth, falls in among thieves, meets the Artful Dodger, and comes under the control of the wicked Fagin. In the end, he defeats a mysterious man named Monk, inherits his rightful fortune, and to boot, lands in a happy family to call his own. Life's twists abound in the life of Oliver Twist with the final scene on pleasant terms.

Everyone loves a happy ending, especially when the beginning was a horrible mess. We are drawn to tales involving the less fortunate, who through dogged determination or just sheer luck, find themselves enjoying life at last. We root for the underdog, for the ones who had little advantage early on in life. If the dastardly villain, who sought to keep the ragged little one in the chains of poverty gets a hardy recompense, well, that's just butter syrup on the figgy pudding. Just ask Pip or little orphan Annie.

Charles Dickens was a master at spinning tales of rags to riches. His stories inspire his readers to persevere in trials because, "we do not know the end of the matter." Hard work and good character are always the path forward, and a stroke of good fortune may be just around the corner. It is interesting to note that Dickens's novels were not written in a vacuum. He lived in dark days, when merry old England wasn't merry at all, especially for the young. In the words of Patricia K. Davis in her book, *A Midnight Carol*, "Children felt old, and the old felt dead; others were too tired to feel anything at all."[84] Dickens's rag to riches stories carried with them a hint of his own life, along with the hopes and aspirations of his times.

Cinderella, or *The Little Glass Slipper*, as it was originally titled, was a classic folktale. The story's earliest known origin travels back to the first century in the story of *Rhodopis*, written by Strabo, a Greek geographer and historian. In it he writes,

> "...*when she was bathing, an eagle snatched one of her sandals from her maid and carried it to Memphis; and while the king was administering justice in the open air, the eagle, when it arrived above his head, flung the sandal into his lap; and the king, stirred by the beautiful shape of the sandal and by the strangeness of the occurrence, sent men in all directions into the country in quest of the woman who wore the sandal; and when she was found in the city of Naucratis, she was brought up to Memphis, became the wife of the king.*" Strabo; "Geography," book 17, 33

Imagine placing your sandal in just the right place to be carried off and dropped at the feet of a king who happens to be looking for a bride. Cinderella was a truly 'rags to riches' story. Misfortune plagued the young maiden at an early age. In the loss of her mother, and then the marriage of her father to a cruel woman, we see a sad turn of events that casts Cinderella into an unfortunate situation. With the arrival of two contemptible half-sisters, life became even more miserable. After the death of her father, the darkness deepened. Forced to wait on her new family hand and foot, she sat in the ashes of her fireplace and hoped for better days.

Undaunted, Cinderella refused to succumb to discouragement. Her heart was heavy, but her dreams would not be denied. Fortunately, better days were brought to bear by a kind fairy godmother and a handsome prince. Oh, the delight of a rags to riches tale. They are the light that spurs us on to a hopeful future.

For all of us the dream of a storybook ending is a precious commodity. The hope of living in a palace of elegance rather than in the squalor of a rickety hut, fuels the heart with hopefulness. "On the wings of my fancy, I can fly anywhere," sang Cinderella. "I can be whatever I want to be." We cling to the hope of an incoming tide that will bring our vessel, laden with diamonds, to its rightful owner. This is why we love rags to riches stories. We live vicariously through these tales of upturns because life *can* be stranger than fiction. The twists and turns of our lives offer opportunities we never could have orchestrated. And so, we live another day to see what will happen.

These stories of the desolate, discovering inherited wealth, also resonate because of a common bond we share. They take us back to a garden, to a tale as old as time, to an ancient linage of extreme poverty. Our communal roots are buried deep within the soil of a great tragedy. We scratch and claw for a place at the table because we were all born in spiritual penury. Ours was a great fall, and all the king's horses, and all the king's men, can't put us back together again. We feel our rags and that is why we long for riches. Our hearts tell us there is something more.

Our minds wonder at the possibility of, "The overman" or superman, as described in Nietzsche's, *Thus spoke Zarathustra*. The idea that mankind can somehow lift himself above his present condition sounds exciting, but in reality, it is always a failed experiment. Unfortunately, the German philosopher's wild brand of free-thinking eventually enslaved him to the point of madness and death. Despite man's best effort to understand his condition, life on a higher plain always seems just beyond his reach.

As a result, we suffer from failed performances throughout life. When the curtain opens, we are instantly filled with the inexplicable fear of failure. This calamity has grounded us in the muck of misery regardless of our successes. The more jingle in our coffers the lonelier we become. The more we achieve the less we are satisfied. Created to fly through the universe directing distant planets and stars, we presently limp upon the ground of our present habitation.

Compared to the riches we were meant to inherit; we muddle through in a ragamuffin world hoping for scraps. Born with two left feet we land on the stage with a thump. Longing for the approval of others, we remain perpetually denied. Time on the stage of life only serves to perpetuate the doom of our disastrous final curtain. The kettle drum of insignificance beats louder as time marches on. The wind section blows incessantly as we are skirted off the stage. We are has-beens before we get warmed up.

"Everything man has ever done is constantly being obliterated; everything a man fights for and lives for passes; he has so many years to live and then it is finished. In true thinking of things as they are, there is always a bedrock of unmitigated sadness. No man who thinks and faces life as it actually is, can be other than pessimistic."[85]

Alas, all is not lost. There is a true rag to riches story available to all, and it is well within our reach. It has been made available through a great sacrifice and simply must be received as an inheritance. However, this wealth has nothing to do with this world. It is vital we understand riches from the perspective of heaven's stage, because at its core, life is a spiritual journey.

The riches promised through the Playwright's grand story are eternal in nature. Subsequently, they cannot be destroyed by fire nor pickpocketed by death. But before these riches can flow into our souls, we must understand how these treasures are brought to bear. To bring us from our rags to his riches, something shocking had to occur. The entire world system had to be set on its ear. Someone had to give up heaven's riches and take on the poverty of Middle earth…

J.R.R. Tolkien in his book, *The Lord of the Rings*, spins a tale of a little hobbit, overlooked for his size, who accomplishes incredible feats of bravery. Frodo Baggins is chosen by the good wizard Gandalf to carry a magical ring to the Cracks of Doom to be destroyed in the very flames from which it was forged. The little hobbit journeys in the company of his fellow hobbits, Sam, Merry, and Pippin on a dangerous journey that proves successful in saving Middle earth from the Dark Lord Sauron. To do this, Frodo and his friends must leave their beloved Shire to save Middle earth.

The Shire, in Tolkien's writings, was a small but beautiful land, fruitful and treasured by its inhabitants. Homes with flower boxes filled with colorful blooms and round doors leading into the sides of grassy mounds, the countryside was a picture of tranquility. Green rolling hills, dotted with quaint villages, the Shire was a paradise for its small citizens. The Hobbits deeply valued their privacy and simple lives.

As for Frodo, all of this was interrupted by the good wizard, Gandalf the Great. The little Hobbit was asked to give up the beauty of the Shire to enter a dangerous world and risk death to rescue the inhabitants of Middle Earth. It is a story rich with the theme of a redemptive hero, who though overlooked, yet achieves the incredible, the destruction of the Ring and the saving of mankind.

There are times when a man will hide his wealth. He may appear as a pauper and really be a prince. When Jesus grew up in Nazareth there was nothing to indicate that he was anything other than an ordinary boy. As a young man, he labored as a humble carpenter in the small town of Nazareth. His family was of average means. However, hidden from the view of family and friends, Jesus was the God who created all things, being eternal with the Father. He came from riches unimaginable to rags painfully apparent as he lived in relative obscurity for the first thirty years of his life.

It is impossible for us to comprehend the glory of Jesus' habitation before he was born in Bethlehem. His riches were immeasurable and his glory beyond the brilliance of all created things. It was the ultimate shock in heaven's court, when earth heard the first cry of the Christ child. Angels no doubt folded their wings as the babe was held close to Mary's breast. Tolkien casts his little Hobbit as a type of Christ, born in humble theater, willing to leave the Shire to destroy that which would eventually destroy mankind. The Ring, a symbol of sin, captivates men with the hope of riches but ultimate brings them into the bondage of rags.

Consider God's great Protagonist, who gave up the wealth of heaven to live in the rags of poverty, to redeem us from our spiritual destitution. Open your heart to the possibility of a truth that sets heaven and earth's stage on fire with the passion of God. Enter a mystery that has astounded the great thinkers of all time. God became flesh in the person of Jesus Christ. Theologians call it the incarnation, God in human form.

Concerning Jesus, the Bible states, "Who, though he was in the form of God, did not count equality with God a thing to be grasped but emptied himself, by taking the form of a servant, being born in the likeness of men."[86] When Jesus entered humanity, he emptied himself of his reputation. This means that he gave up his divine privileges. In no way did he give up his deity, for that would have been impossible. God can be nothing less and remain fully himself. He maintained all his divine attributes, and yet, for us, he decided to step off his throne and take upon himself the form of a servant. Jesus went from riches to rags. He lived a sinless life to qualify himself as the spotless Lamb, to offer the perfect sacrifice for our sins. He did this to provide for us the riches of salvation. This is where our rags to riches story begins.

The importance of understanding the poverty that Christ embraced cannot be underestimated as it is encapsulated in one astounding declaration in the New Testament. "For our sake he made him to be sin who knew no sin, so that in him we might become the righteousness of God."[87] Jesus, who knew no sin was made to be sin. This truth stops the show and calls all creation to attention. The Holy One, who dwells in unapproachable light, entered the darkness of humanity. He came from heaven to enrich us by taking on our spiritual destitution. He entered the extreme crucible of poverty, which was the cross, to die in our place.

Jesus became a sin sacrifice that we might escape our spiritual poverty and be adopted as sons and daughters. This thought is beyond our ability to comprehend. It must be received by faith. A child gazing into the night sky doesn't understand what he sees, but he still looks on it in wonder. He doesn't question its reality. Christ forfeited his riches to rescue us from our rags.

On heaven's stage, the rags to riches narrative is the major theme. Receiving this truth causes the disappointment of our days to give way to the hope of an eternal tomorrow. Life takes on a paradigm shift in regard to what we consider valuable. Let's dig deeper into the redemptive narrative.

When we discover what true riches are, our definition of success changes dramatically. In fact, our way of seeing life is turned upside down. We begin to realize we have propped our ladder against the wrong wall. We have chased chickens and ignored the golden goose. Treasures in this world become fodder. Money, fame, and power are nothing more than chalk marks that can be quickly washed away by the next rainstorm. The true riches, peace, joy, and contentment are intangible.

Happily, we find ourselves walking to the beat of a much different drum. Rather than being fixated upon our own dog and pony show, our eyes are redirected to the unseen, ever present Scriptwriter. Over time we begin to release our lives, allowing him to make the grand decisions that determine our life's path. Jesus said that in order to find your life, you must lose it. This abiding truth has been the delightful discovery of saints throughout the ages and especially in the life of the great lawgiver of Israel.

The path of Moses' life was played out in two acts with a long intermission. His rags to riches story may appear to be quite the opposite. Starting out in the palace of Egypt seems like a fast track to the top. Riches, well in hand, it appeared Moses would never experience rags. However, God had other plans. A desert is where he would eventually land, and that was exactly where God wanted him. Let's track the Playwright's movements in his life.

Moses was well on his way to top billing in the country of Egypt, which was strange indeed seeing that he was born a Hebrew slave. Adopted by Pharaoh's daughter, by a miracle float down the Nile past hungry crocs, he became the apple of her eye. While Jewish babies all around him were being thrown in the river, baby Moses was nurtured and cared for by his own mother, Jochebed.

At some point, early in his life, he was brought into the Egyptian palace. Raised in Pharaoh's court he received the best of training to prepare him for his future seat on the throne. The riches of the greatest country in the world, at that time, were at his fingertips. Power beyond imagination awaited Moses as he worked through each day in the lap of luxury. The first forty years of his life were a dream come true, but then came the nightmare. In a moment of anger, Moses forfeited his future and ended up in a forty year intermission. It was an interruption that played right into God's narrative. This is how the story unfolded.

Moses was living in two worlds. One look in the mirror told him he was not a true Egyptian. He was undeniably Jewish. He lived in the palace while his brethren were slaves. He was pampered while they were being whipped. The dichotomy of his dual citizenship, no doubt, perplexed and agitated him. Then came the day everything changed.

As Moses walked past a group of slaves, he watched a fellow Jew being abused by his slave master. Fury arose within him, and he killed the Egyptian. Fearful of the consequences, Moses buried the man in the sand. However, a fellow Jew had watched the event and threatened to expose him. And thus, the man, who hoped to be Pharoah one day, walked down a dusty, dirt road. Out into the desert he went, to become a herder of sheep for a man named Jethro. Eventually, Moses married Jethro's daughter and was brought into the family business. Welcome to life's twists and turns.

Swallowed in obscurity, Moses spent the next forty years learning one very important lesson. By his own strength he could not rescue his fellow Jews. Deliverance had to be the work of God alone. The performance he would eventually give on earth's greatest stage had to be orchestrated by the Director. Moses was not ready. He needed training in the desert of hard knocks. He was set aside for a season, for a very specific reason.

Act Two began in a very unusual way. God appeared to Moses in a burning bush. It was a supernatural event. The bush, fueled by the combustion of deity, refused to burn up. As he turned aside to witness this phenomenon, God spoke to him out of the bush. Moses was told to go barefoot because the ground he was standing on was holy. It was the ground that was holy, not just the bush. The common dirt under his feet had become hallowed as the natural was set ablaze with the supernatural. It was just another day in the wilderness, but it changed Moses forever.

We were created from the dust of the earth. "Then the LORD God formed the man of dust from the ground and breathed into his nostrils the breath of life, and the man became a living creature."[88] It is the fusion of the creature with the divine that sets us apart from the rest of creation. The glory of man's making is God breathing into us the human spirit. The heavenly making its home in the earthly. "But we have this treasure in jars of clay, to show that the surpassing power belongs to God and not to us."[89]

On heaven's stage there is no separation between the secular and the sacred. It is the Director's great joy to impart the eternal into the temporal. The fire God desires to burn within us does not destroy us, it enlightens us to see an unseen world. Moses began to see all those wasted years as a preparatory phase for his moment on holy ground. God has not forgotten him as he saw the divine hand guiding him. As a result, his life was devoted to a new mission. Moses would be used of God in the deliverance of his people.

When the Director appears, our lives are transformed. The ordinary days become a continual sacred enterprise. All of life, with every precious experience, is heaven's stage. Heaven is not in a faraway place shrouded by a hazy mist. It is all around us because God is ever present in our desert wanderings. He does not reveal himself in grand entrances announced beforehand, but in the ordinary, unexpected times. We go from rags to riches when we acknowledge the One who went from riches to rags. It is his riches alone that sets us free. "On the wings of *his* fancy I can fly anywhere, I can be whatever *he* wants me to be." (emphasis mine) Sometimes where he calls us surprises us.

Gary and Dena Pate were married for 39 years, with two grown children and six wonderful grandchildren, when God called them to move to the country of Ecuador. Gary writes in his own words…

"I didn't finish high school, and I have never been to seminary. I took my first mission trip 35 years ago and on the way back God began to deal with my heart about missions. We had small children at the time. My wife and I began to pray and for next twenty-one years we asked God to use us in the capacity of full-time missions. I was in the business world at the time and my wife was a nurse at a hospital in Jacksonville, Florida. We got two weeks of vacation every year, and we gave one of those weeks almost every year to go on a foreign missions' trip. We were very involved in our church. We've done everything from medical missions to construction and evangelism. We have been in about twelve different countries over the years.

In 2010, after 21 years of praying, we were on a mission's trip in the jungle of Ecuador when the Holy Spirit spoke to my heart and said, "now is the time". We came back to Jacksonville, and we sold everything. We resigned our jobs and raised enough money to go to language school. Our friends thought we were mad. At this time, we were empty nesters. We had a six-digit income with no debt except the mortgage on our home. From the world's viewpoint we were flying high. When we left the country, I was 49 years old.

We started working with children up in the Andes mountains of Ecuador where we would drive to nine different rural villages. Most of the children and the mothers lived in mud huts at a chilly 10,000 foot elevation. It's not easy living in Ecuador as it is a very different culture. Dena and I don't have a church family, nor do we have any blood relatives in Ecuador. Some mornings I wake up, brush my teeth, look in the mirror and think, *what in the world am I doing here.* I think about these children memorizing the Bible, and I realize that this is what makes it all worthwhile. We are giving them God's word which is the only thing that will matter."

The Pate's story can be retold countless times as those who follow the Director's cues give up what they cannot keep to gain what they cannot lose. They happily forfeited a comfortable retirement, including travel and being close to family, to minister to the children of Ecuador. In the eyes of the world, they exchanged easy street for muddy trails in the mountains of Ecuador. In reality, they choose the true riches of heaven over the rags of this world. Eternity will reveal the wisdom of their decision.

Life lived from a purely rational standpoint is exasperating. It is vexing. We attempt to make sense of the nonsensible. We cry foul at every turn. Stacking the blocks in a perfect row, we convince ourselves that they will never fall but they do. "Then I said in my heart, 'What happens to the fool will happen to me also. Why then have I been so very wise?' And I said in my heart that this also is vanity."[90] It is also futile to look to any government for help. "So, the law is paralyzed, and justice never goes forth. For the wicked surround the righteous, so justice goes forth perverted."[91] The brute wins the day while the honest bloke goes hungry for justice. "Truth forever on the scaffold, wrong forever on the throne."[92] There's a part of the equation we must be missing because we were created as thinking people, and life, most of the time, doesn't add up.

A Series of Unfortunate Events, written by Daniel Handler, a.k.a. Lemony Snicket, chronicles the sad story of three orphans, Violet, Klaus, and Sunny. Known as the Baudelaire children, their propensity for bad luck knew no bounds. They were kind and witty, and yet, the sun never seemed to shine on their day at the beach. After learning of the tragic death of their parents, and the eventual inheritance due the oldest child, Violet, the trio sets off on a series of adventures with the evil Count Olaf hard on their trail. For the Baudelaire children, unfortunate events are around every turn.

It is a series of thirteen books each containing thirteen chapters. The number thirteen seems fitting. In the last book, titled, *The End*, there are 14 chapters breaking from Handler's practice of thirteen per book. Elements of resolution fill this chapter as questions are answered, and destinies are fulfilled. Things begin to make sense for the Baudelaire children. It is the 14th chapter of our lives that counts. When we enter heaven's stage, it doesn't necessarily end our own series of unfortunate events, but it does begin to put them in the proper perspective. What is going on around us is of little consequence, when compared to what is going on within us. When we are looking at life from God's viewpoint, even the unfortunate events are seen to have a place and a purpose.

The positioning of stage left, or stage right, is from the outlook of the actors, not the view of the audience. In essence, the theater goer sees everything backwards. If the script directs an actress to exit "stage right" the crowd watches her walk off toward the left side of the theater. Orientation in life is vital, for without it we are always going in the wrong direction.

Only those who stand on heaven's stage see life in proper focus. When Paul arrived in Thessalonica, he caused quite a stir by simply preaching the gospel. He was brought before the local magistrates with this accusation, "These men who have turned the world upside down have come here also,"[93] That's an interesting charge to level against Paul and his compadres. Those men were actually turning the world right side up. They were helping people reject the rags of what they thought life was all about and receive the true riches of a relationship with God. Their entire value system was readjusted.

We did not choose our character nor the events that shaped our lives. However, whether born in a mansion or a hut, we all entered life covered in the rags of sin. By the grace of God, we have all been offered eternal salvation. We have been handed a script and offered a place on the most glorious stage known to man. The Scriptwriter awaits our entrance through the door of redemption. He longs to beautifully blend us into his story. He desires we see the riches of this world as rags and cast them aside for the treasures that are eternal.

CHAPTER 8

Stage Fright

Stage fright is real. Just ask anyone who has ever stood before a crowd whose faces resembled cracked plaster of Paris. To sing, dance or deliver a line before a live audience can be debilitating. Sweaty palms, a difficulty to breathe, and dizziness are all included in this wonderfully horrible experience. Merriam-Webster defines stage fright as, "nervousness felt when appearing before an audience." Simple enough, but the actual experience feels more complicated.

The term, *stage fright*, was first used in 1876 by Mark Twain in his novel, *The Adventures of Tom Sawyer*. As Tom attempts to deliver the speech, "Give me Liberty or give me Death," before a school assembly he suddenly gives way to nerves and becomes a pile of mush. "A ghastly stage-fright seized him, his legs quaked under him, and he was like to choke. True, he had the manifest sympathy of the house, but he had the house's silence too, which was even worse than its sympathy. The master frowned, and this completed the disaster. Tom struggled awhile and then retired, utterly defeated. There was a weak attempt at applause, but it died early."[94] Between liberty and death poor Tom yearned for the former but was afflicted with the latter. Not even Huck Finn could rescue him.

However, people have experienced stage fright long before 1876, but that was the year we gave it a name. Interestingly, it was the same year that the word *tight-lipped* was introduced into the English language.

Unfortunately, this dreaded phenomenon is more common than we think. Most of us avoid the stage like the plague.

Joan Acocella writes in *The New Yorker*, dated July 27th, 2015, "Stage fright has not been heavily studied, which is strange because, as Solovitch tells us, it is common not only among those who make their living on the stage but among the rest of us, too. In 2012, two researchers at the University of Nebraska-Omaha, Karen Dwyer and Marlina Davidson, administered a survey to 815 college students, asking them to select their three greatest fears from a list that included, among other things, heights, flying, financial problems, deep water, death, and 'speaking before a group.' Speaking before a group beat out all the others, even death."[95]

In some cases, stage fright can lead to stage flight. Acocella continues, "In 1989, Daniel Day-Lewis, playing the title role in Richard Eyre's production of "Hamlet" at London's National Theatre, turned on his heel in the middle of the show and walked off the stage, never to return. (In the 26 years since then, he has acted only in movies.) "I had nothing in me, nothing to say, nothing to give," he said. Others stay, but only by force of sheer, grinding will." Ibid

Even the great English actor, Lawrence Olivier, was afflicted with stage fright while in his fifties. The agony lasted five years before he eventually conquered it.[96]

However, the famous are not the only ones afflicted by stage fright. We have all felt its icy fingers, its debilitating grip, and not necessarily before a crowd. In pivotal moments, when we should have acted, we remained in the shadows. The unexpected circumstance arrived and everything within us screamed to speak up, and there we stood, frozen in fear. Perhaps, we were considering the fallout of our word or deed rather than the good it could have accomplished.

Moses was the first recorded case of stage fright in world history. His fear of speaking before an audience was so bad that even a burning bush couldn't convince him to walk out onto an Egyptian stage. He finally convinced the Lord to allow his younger brother, Aaron, to accompany him in confronting Pharoah's court.

There are more examples from the Bible. The Lord had to cook Gideon's supper with fire from a rock and dampen a fleece before he came out of hiding. Jonah sailed in the opposite direction when God called him to Nineveh's stage. Elijah brought down fire from heaven but then hid in a cave when it was time for an encore featuring Jezebel. Much later, God warned his prophet Jeremiah not to be afraid of the faces of those in the audience.[97]

Regardless of whether stage fright is caused by our insecurities, or born of past failures, it is an ugly reminder of our cowardness; our decision to play it safe. We clammed up, and the opportunity to create our own dynamic in the scene passed to someone else. We walked away thinking, why didn't I speak, why didn't I say my piece? We should have told them how we felt but didn't. Unfortunately, thinking I love you, is not the same as saying, I love you. There are further reasons why we struggle with this debilitating beast.

Harry Clay Miner was the founder of the world's first theater chain. He was a New York City policeman, US congressman, and printer, however, his most famous establishment was Miner's Bowery Theatre, established in 1878. The theater boasted such acts as Eddie Cantor, Al Jolson, W.C. Fields, who was then a juggler, and A.O. Dunkin (vaudeville's first ventriloquist). His son, Tom, instituted the theatre's amateur night, which met biweekly, and became famous for its innovation of "getting the hook." If the act was suffering, and needed to be put to death, the crowd began to chant, "Get the hook!" A large shepherd's crook was then used to jerk the flailing act off the stage. The practice became a part of pop culture being popularized by *Looney Tunes* and *The Muffet show*.[98]

Tom Miner's creation of 'the hook' is now galvanized in our minds as a psychological thumbs down on our attempts to live life with risk. In the words of Joe Cocker, "What would you do if I sang out of tune? Would you stand up and walk out on me?" Again, we fear the hook. The heavy weight of judgement from the peanut gallery hangs around our necks like an anvil. It keeps from the 'daring things.' Nevertheless, the words of Joseph Chilton Pearce ring true, "To live a creative life, we must lose the fear of being wrong."[99]

Fear keeps us grounded when we should be flying. We prune our feathers and stretch our wings and never spread them to soar. Peer pressure afflicts us our whole lives. To *think* we can accomplish something is the first step toward achieving our dreams. To reject the fear of the big, bad, hook is the second. Push on my fellow warrior into something new. If the Director is leading, you have nothing to fear, and always remember, you perform before an audience of One. And if perhaps you do fail, he will pick you up, brush you off, and send you back out onto his stage.

Still, stage fright does seem to grow as we move through life. "Life's but a walking shadow, a poor player that struts and frets his hour upon the stage, and then is heard no more: it is a tale told by an [fool], full of sound and fury, signifying nothing." Macbeth (5.5.8) This line out of Shakespeare is depressing at best, but it sadly, at times, mirrors our lives.

With age comes a track record of failed moments and embarrassing situations that we sometimes brought upon ourselves. We become "walking shadows." Shell-shocked into submission to those who tell us to know our place. Consequently, we risk little and accomplish less and less. Burned by ruthless critics who tell us to stay in our lane, we willingly agree to stay off the stage of life.

As a result, there are very few that are charging out onto the stage and singing their song with gusto. Clinging to a thick, musty stage curtain, we break out in a cold sweat when we should be launching out into new venues and adventures. Presented with clear opportunities, we cower behind excuses. "The sluggard says, "There is a lion in the road! There is a lion in the streets!"[100] Stage fright is a beast that lives in the avenues of our mind. Someone or something has pulled the plug on our marquee lights.

Regrettably, we practiced the art of restraint. We learn the importance of wearing a mask. Hiding behind a false persona, we work hard to keep others at bay. We simply fear the possibility of failure and rejection. Charles Swindoll, in his book, *Dropping Your Guard*, writes this, "There is just one major difficulty in this mask-wearing game, it isn't real. It therefore forces us to skate rather than relate. It promotes a phony-baloney, make-a-good impression attitude instead of an honest realism that relieves and frees. What's worse, as we hide the truth behind a veneer polished to a high gloss, we become lonely instead of understood and loved for who we are. And the most tragic part of all is that the longer we do it, the better we get at it— and the more alone we remain in our hidden world of fear, pain, anger, insecurity, and grief- all those normal and natural emotions we hesitate to admit but that prove we are human."[101] Our sheltering mechanism, which we have developed our entire lives, does not disintegrate in a moment. Like the actors and actresses of ancient Greece we choose the mask that best fits the present scene. It takes time and rugged practice to become comfortable in our own skin and be ourselves around other people, but it is possible.

Granted, there are times to conceal our true thoughts and emotions but as a rule it is unhealthy and exhausting. Merton once said, "Be yourself; there is very little chance of being anyone else."[102] If we are, 'fearfully and wonderfully made,' then why fear the audience. The pastor of Hope City Church in Indianapolis, Indiana reminds us, "Masks make shallow what God has intended to be deep. Everything in our life gets cheated when we choose to hide behind our masks."[103]

The reason we hesitate is both subtle and powerful. The origin of stage fright began in the garden of Eden but quickly accelerated after the great flood of Noah's day. On the heels of the flood, as mankind re-populated the earth, a new evil surfaced. The psyche of man was deeply affected as the story of the world-wide destruction was told and retold. And instead of acknowledging the righteous judgment of God, mankind, instead, developed a deeper rebellion toward God. Mutiny filled their hearts. The great tower of Babel was built to reach to the heavens in direct defiance of the Creator. The construction of the colossal edifice screamed; *You will never drown us again in a flood. You cannot touch us with your judgment, because we will simply climb higher into our tower.* It was the response of fools.

Mankind began to project his own greatness over the majesty of God and a man named Nimrod blazed the trail. The Bible refers to him as a "great hunter before the Lord."[104] There were millions living on the Earth at the time of the flood, and yet, this title was the first to be given to any man. This designation, a mighty man, seems harmless on its surface, but when we dig deeper, an evil emerges that chills the bone. Clearly a new era had arrived.

Ever since Nimrod, humanity has desired greatness in their individual and corporate pursuits. Their lust for power, and hence, control knows no bounds. However, it is his drive for greatness, apart from his God, that produces a man's deepest insecurity. The individuality of man was never meant for the limelight. Man was destined for greatness, but only in concert with his Creator. The very spotlight he desires becomes the cause for his stage fright.

Nonetheless, of all the actors that have appeared on heaven's stage, there *is* one who has stormed that sacred theater and needs to, "get the hook!" It is Satan, and in his case, stage fright is justified. His "hook" began with a mortal wound in the garden and was fulfilled on the cross. Lucifer's time on the stage is limited, and he knows it. Jesus said, "Now is the judgment of this world; now will the ruler of this world be cast out."[105] "And he said to them, "I saw Satan fall like lightning from heaven."[106]

In the book of Isaiah, Satan is paraded to his doom. As he passes in front of the rulers of the nations, they are astonished at his appearance, having finally seen him who lived in the shadows. "Those who see you will stare at you and ponder over you: Is this the man who made the earth tremble, who shook kingdoms."[107] The "hook" will seal his doom in a lake of fire. "And the devil who had deceived them was thrown into the lake of fire and sulfur where the beast and the false prophet were, and they will be tormented day and night forever and ever."[108] Good riddance to our enemy.

Concerning our present stage, we have nothing to fear. The devil cannot derail our performance. To the Romans, who were a conquering people, Paul wrote, "The God of peace will soon crush Satan under your feet." Jesus promised, "Behold, I have given you authority to tread on serpents and scorpions, and over all the power of the enemy, and nothing shall hurt you."[109] Satan still roams the earth. Peter reminds us, "Be sober-minded; be watchful. Your adversary the devil prowls around like a roaring lion, seeking someone to devour."[110] John encourages us in light of this, "Little children, you are from God and have overcome them, for he who is in you is greater than he who is in the world."[111]

There is, however, a further cause for stage fright. Ellen Terry, a respected and beloved actress in her time, suffered from the clawing effects of stage fright in 1861. Given five different parts to play simultaneously she crumbled under the pressure. Describing the horrors of the experience she wrote, "You feel as if a centipede, all of those feet have been carefully iced, has begun to run about in the roots of your hair. Then it seems as if somebody has cut the muscles at the back of your knees. As your mouth slowly opens, no sound comes out. It was torture, like nothing else in the world."[112]

The beauty of heaven's stage is that we are only given one part. We are told to follow the Director. Jesus told us to come to him, and he would give us rest. He said, "Follow me, and I will make you fishers of men."[113] Everything on heaven's stage flows out of rest. Our responsibility in life boils down to one essential ingredient, a continual focus on the Director. In our interaction with other members of the cast, the question should never arise within us, "how shall I play this part?" Our dominating should be, "how can I be a blessing to my fellow stage member." We integrate into the daily performance best by holding others in highest esteem. As we focus on Jesus Christ, our love for others only grows deeper. Valuing people, and ourselves, also means never comparing ourselves to them.

Moses was a tough act to follow. Imagine peeping out from the curtain and seeing the Red Sea part or your protégé walking down from Mt. Sinai with his face shining with glory. It's enough to send you begging for your job back selling tickets. However, God never required his protégé, Joshua, to do such things. He never asked him to strike a rock so water would pour from it. At the outset of Israel entering Canaan land, the Director told him, quite bluntly, that Moses had exited stage left, he was dead, and that he was now to lead the nation. Every man walks his own path, and it is foolish to compare ourselves to anyone else, because God has made us unique. The Lord told Joshua to look ahead and leave Moses where he belonged, as an inspiration, not a model. It was *his* time on the stage, and God had equipped him, as he does us.

A young pastor was attempting to find his way in the pulpit. He tried to imitate some of his favorite preachers by using their style and inflections. After failing miserably, he was discouraged. His wife wisely asked him, "Why don't you just try being you?" I am grateful Chuck Swindoll took her advice.

After a long and dark journey into the realm of stage fright, what is the answer to ridding ourselves from its clutches. It's really quite simple.

When we embrace heaven's stage, the fear of performing evaporates. When we discover that we are deeply loved by the Director, regardless of our performance, we relax. There is nothing left to prove. When our eyes are focused on the Playwright, and not ourselves, we become absent in the room, or on the stage. We perform well because we don't know we're performing. We become spontaneous because being unprompted is the nature of love. We do not plan on saying words of adoration to those we love; it just flows out of us.

In daily life there are no lines to memorize, but only a series of spontaneous moments with opportunities to strengthen our fellow man. Being genuine must be natural. If you have to write out words of affection, and then coldly read them from memory, it snuffs the candle flame of authenticity. A heart that is fueled with the love of God does not have to be driven by a script. Stage fright ceases to exist in the heart that is centered on the love and full acceptance of the Director. In fact, we grow to adore his story and naturally embrace heaven's stage. So, reject fear, and dance your dance with everything within you. There are no hooks on heaven's stage, only applause.

CHAPTER 9

Breaking the Fourth Wall

B reaking the fourth wall occurs when an actress or actor leaves the scene and addresses the audience directly...

The house lights dim as the curtain slowly rises. Flats appear presenting a barren landscape broken only by the occasional homestead and surrounding farms. Domestic animals dot the hillside. The crowd settles into their seats, anxious to see what will become of the man and his family. The previous scene had begun with a rich man at peace and ended with a celestial challenge between two opposing forces. The rich man had been unknowingly placed in the crosshairs of a cosmic struggle between God and Satan.

Sheep are heard bleating in the distance as a pair of camels scroll awkwardly across the stage coming dangerously close to falling into the orchestra pit. The Director and the musical ensemble breathe a sigh of relief as the camels move stage right. A man walks out from stage left and kneels near the apron. Lifting his face to the heavens, he speaks silently into the air. The crowd leans forward in their seats trying to hear what he is saying. The prayerful man appears confident, and peaceful.

The spotlight dims as new flats roll onto the stage revealing herds of cattle and sheep grazing in the lowlands. A pair of oxen are plowing next to a small herd of donkeys. The stage becomes crowded as men appear, brushing out the rough hide of the camels. On the opposite side of the stage, laughter erupts from a large gathering in a home. A thunderous sound explodes from the orchestra pit, as an approaching storm threatens to descend on the unsuspecting family. The man near the apron keeps praying.

The dust from a band of marauding thieves rises from the slopes above one of the farms. The music from the orchestra pit begins its crescendo. The crowd awaits the crisis that will launch the unsuspecting protagonist on his journey of discovery. The constant beat of a heavy kettle drum fills the hall with a sense of impending calamity and doom. The beat increases in speed promising a short but powerful scene, filled with the pathos of life. The man prays with great passion. The Director raises his hands to bring the scene to its dramatic conclusion when suddenly, a frantic man charges onto the stage from the back curtain. Waving his hands he brings the orchestra to a grinding halt. The French horn sours its last note.

The audience is stunned and confused. Is this a part of the performance? Why has this man chosen to break the 4th wall? They scan the program as a buzzing murmur fills the theater. Walking briskly out onto center stage, a man dressed in cattlemen's clothing frantically motions for the Director to stop the scene.

"Wait, wait, wait! I cannot stand by and allow these nightly exercises in insanity to proceed any further. Before we destroy this man's life again for no good reason, I have something to say to the Playwright. Is he in the building tonight?"

"Walter, he's in the building every night," whispers a young lad nearby. "The Director *is* the Playwright."

"I beg your pardon. No matter how much time I spend in this theater I keep forgetting that the same man who is directing the play wrote it."

Security guards rush onto the stage to carry Walter away. The crowd shifts nervously in their seats. How dare this man interrupt the performance. The lines have been written. The plot has been carefully constructed, and the actors have been cast. The nerve of this lonely one-line actor to question the Playwright in the midst of the performance. The story cannot be altered by anyone, for any reason. "Fall in line donkey boy and be grateful that you have the one line you have been blessed to deliver," shouts someone in the crowd. Walter begins to be carried off the stage.

"Stop," shouts the Director as he rises from his chair.

The audience sits with bated breath awaiting the Director's fury. Walter stands defiantly having pulled himself free from the guards.

"Go ahead and speak your mind young man. Since you have already interrupted the scene, you may now address the audience and myself. The stage is yours. I will listen to your concerns."

The audience and actors stare at the Director in unbelief. He appeared moments before to be in total control of his theater. Why would he allow anyone to question him, much less during the performance. The Director, sensing their thoughts, motions for the audience to sit down. He seems strangely pleased with Walter's boldness.

The guards slowly back away as a spotlight beams down onto the man. All the other actors and actresses on the stage sit down, waiting to hear what the mutineer has to say. Some seem perturbed that anyone would interrupt the performance. Others appear grateful that he is voicing his objection to the story. They also were thinking the play was too depressive and dark to be enjoyed by the performers or the audience.

At first, Walter appears stunned, but then, regaining his composure, he squares himself toward the Director. His voice trembles at first. "I dare say I have studied the script more than most who stand on this stage, and I feel as though I have legitimate concerns that need to be addressed."

The Director smiles.

Walter continued, "I must first say that I am a thinking person who refuses to be led about with a ring in my nose. I know what is right, and I know what is wrong, and what you have written is monstrously criminal. I would have never written a script like this. I would have never destroyed a man's entire life in a day."

The audience jumps to its feet in defense of the Playwright as the guards reappear to take the man away. Some head for the exits only to be told to go back to their seats by the Director. Others begin to shout at the man.

"Heretic! Fool! How dare you question the Playwright's story." A nearby actress can take no more, "You can be easily replaced. I wish to hear no more of such treachery."

The Playwright leans forward.

"I want to hear more."

Walter stares into the eyes of the Playwright. His words are so softly spoken that most did not hear him. A flicker of brightness fills the Director's eyes, as he gently smiles. He appears to be a man who has been waiting for such a question, waiting for the barebones honesty of his troupe. The Director almost seems relieved that someone has finally voiced the concern that most harbored silently.

"Excuse me. What did you say?" asks Walter.

"I said speak on. I wish to know what is on your heart and perhaps how *you* would have written the scene."

It's a trap. He's setting me up, Walter thought. *He'll use my own words at my trial and execution. As soon as I'm done, the crowd will lynch me to the delight of my fellow actors.*

"Go on, tell me what's on your mind. You have no reason to fear. I really want to know what causes you such distress."

The man clears his throat.

"Very well. My difficulty began in the opening scene. The king of the cosmos allows the villain of the ages into his court for the purpose of challenging him to a fight. The antagonist should have been sent packing. And then to boot, the king throws one of his own faithful followers under the oxen cart."

"Go on."

Walter's mouth was working faster than his brain. He knew he was digging his own grave, but he was in too deep to stop now. The expression on the Playwright's face filled him with questions. He seemed genuinely interested. *It is a ruse.* Nevertheless, he continued.

"Why would you write a story placing a good man in utter vulnerability to a far superior being? This is the very source of my complaint. The king of heaven is supposed to be righteous, and yet, he is the very one who initiates the downfall of this good man. You have pulled the king off his throne and made him look like a foolish schoolboy. Inviting the villain to wreak havoc in a mortal's life is like offering a bone to a dog and then expecting the bone to fight back. In your story the king becomes the villain, and the evil one appears justified in his actions toward the unsuspecting man. You really shot yourself in the foot from the very beginning of your play."

"Hold up. The king didn't offer his enemy a bone; he threw out a challenge in order to prove a point," replied the Director.

"Have you considered that a man's life hangs in the balance? What point is important enough to destroy his life? And then the villain suggests that if the king simply removes his protective covering over the man, that would be sufficient. But then, shock upon shock, the king hands his servant over to his enemy for the purpose of… what did you say, 'to prove a point'? Really!"

"You make all good, valid points. I understand your concerns, but I think you are missing the big picture. Walter, you are watching a single tree fall and missing the forest that will grow as a result. Do you know why I wrote this play in the first place?"

"I don't have a clue. I can't get past scene one. A tiny ant is going to be stepped on by the very essence of evil, and a supposedly benevolent sovereign is allowing it. For the sake of proving some point, an innocent man is going to be bull rushed, all in one day. One day!"

"Innocent," says the Director, as he rubs his chin. "That's an interesting way to describe any man, don't you think? What made you think the man was innocent?"

"Oh, let me think. How did the king of heaven describe him from the script? He was blameless, upright, reverent to God. Turning away from evil comes to mind. Sounds pretty innocent to me."

"Alright, I could see how you could possibly interpret all those statements to define innocence, but what makes you think that his good attributes would prevent the things that will befall him?"

"Because everything happens because of our actions. We reap what he sow. I think the king said that somewhere. You paint a rosy picture of the man, and then you tear the canvas to shreds. It is all immoral."

His fellow actors and actresses on the stage draw back expecting the anger of the Director to flare up, but no such explosion comes. Instead, another settled expression of kinship emerges across the Playwright's brow. He is obviously enjoying the exchange.

"That sounds like a dull play, Walter. No surprises, no unforeseen twists. Without a turn, the story spudders along and ends up on a dusty bookshelf or played out in an empty theater. Look at the crowd behind me. Without a crisis there is no adventure. A knight without a dragon to slay is a hay throwing peasant. Do much writing, Walter?"

"I'm impressed you know my name."

"Why wouldn't I?"

"Because I deliver one measly line, that no one will remember, in a sad and pathetic story."

"I make it my business to know all my actors and actresses' names. Every one of them is important to me."

Attempting to hide his emotions, Walter turns away in anger.

"And as far as people remembering your line, Walter, this tale will be retold a thousand times in millions of people's lives. It will be acted out, in various forms, in theaters across the globe. You are a part of a story that will be one of great encouragement down through the ages. Now, back to your trouble with my script."

"Weren't you listening? You blindsided the man. He was a good father and, by all accounts, a good husband. He had raised his children to adulthood. They were all successful and happy. The man had grown his business to the point where he had employed many happy workers. His workers seemed content with their wages and his treatment of them. He even prayed to the king of heaven for protection and blessing, which was apparently a waste of time. And then, without warning, the king of heaven allows his enemy to take it all away. Again, IN A DAY!"

"Are you alone in this assessment?" asked the Director.

The cattlemen begin to shuffle. Three men and a woman slowly step from behind a thick curtain.

"Ah, my other messengers of tragedy," observes the Director as he smiles. "You three also have trouble with the script?"

"Beg your pardon, sir..."

"I believe you deliver the news concerning the loss of the man's camels," interrupted the Director. "You, standing behind him, you're the woman who announces the destruction of the sheep by fire from heaven."

"Yes."

"Go ahead, young man."

"Yes, sir. I mean your high and lifted up..."

"Oh, just say what you need to say, Charlie. I haven't been struck down with lightning yet," said Walter, not attempting to hide his frustration.

"The night is young," mumbles the woman behind him.

The man continues, "Sir, I just think you could have saved my co-workers from being killed. I mean, a camel's just a camel, but you went a little too far, in my humble opinion, by killing off my crew." Pausing, he looks over at the guards and then proceeds. "When I think of that poor man and the news I must deliver, it just makes my stomach sick. Of course, all those decisions are yours to make. You *are* the Playwright. I just feel a little uncomfortable with the path you have chosen."

Walter rolls his eyes as the woman steps forward.

"Mr. Director, as you just mentioned, I deliver the news to the man concerning his flock of sheep being fried with a lightning strike. 7000 sheep if I am correct."

"You are correct."

"Well, that's a lot a smoked mutton if you ask me."

The boys on the catwalk begin to chuckle.

"Quiet up there," said the Director. "Continue."

"I mean, sir, why not blacken only one hundred? By changing that narrative, the king of heaven might appear gentler and kinder to animals. As far as my fellow sheep herders go, I'm fine with the volts passing through their worthless bodies. I mean, I have coworkers on my day job that need to be fried to a crispy brown. They're lazy, you understand."

The boys upstairs struggle to contain themselves.

The fourth actor steps forward and scratches his chin. After adjusting his glasses, he begins.

"Excuse me. You're the son's servant, aren't you?"

"Yes. And thank you for choosing me for the role. I've been out of work for months and the bills are piling up. I mean, just the other day my wife was telling me…"

"Seriously! This is *not* what we talked about backstage. Just spill the beans before I have a stroke," shouted Walter.

"Well, sir, there is nothing more important than a man's family. I suggest you destroy their house and leave the kids untouched. I mean, maybe a few bumps and bruises. This would improve the script ten-fold. No pun intended. Get it, ten kids?"

"I get it." The Director smiled.

Walter grunted. As the other actors step back behind the curtain, Walter continues to stand alone on the stage before the Playwright. Clearing his throat he continues.

"I agree with my fellow thespians. You are too extreme. If you must, then simply cripple the oldest, the first-born son. I think it would have the same effect as killing all of them. The others could weep over their injured brother. To wipe out all his children with a single blow is to alienate every parent in the audience. If you must kill them, then perhaps, have them die peacefully in their sleep. The thought of a house collapsing on these celebrating siblings is too much for the mind to absorb. The theater critics will eat this up and destroy your good name."

The Director looks at Walter thoughtfully before commenting.

"I understand that difficult news is hard to bear. There are times, though, that misfortune is thrust upon the sons of men. Tragedy befalls all human lives. Life altering moments are a part of the human experience. A land without rain is called a desert, my friend. What I am attempting to expose through this play is a deep-seated belief that the calamities of life have no purpose, and that heartache would not occur if God really cared."

Walters appears perplexed.

"But that is my very point. What happens to this man originates in the courts of heaven by a sovereign king who should have protected his follower. This story will destroy the possibility of the sons of men in reaching out to this king in heaven. Through your writing you have brought the king down and made him appear as if he were a celestial chess player using a terrestrial board. The characters appear in the story as nothing but pawns and rooks in the king's hand.

"It's not as simple as that."

A long and purposeful pause was followed by Walter's persistent line of questioning.

"Look, I understand tragedy. Life is not going to be a bed of roses. Along with the sunshine there has to be a little rain sometimes, goes the song. I get it. Again, what bothers me is the way you have characterized the king. Heaven in league with Hell. A king, arm wrestling with a lowly gutter rat. It is like Gandalf joining Sauron to destroy Frodo. It's akin to the Wizard of Oz aiding and abetting the Wicked Witch of the West. Poor Dorothy. Poor unsuspecting man in the desert."

"Go on. I'm listening. I love a thinking mind."

"Think about the opening scene. The king approaches his nemesis by first asking him where he has been. A little boring, but I'll go with it. The villain answers, 'Up and down, to and fro on the earth.' Apparently, he was simply touring the countryside. He's making conversation. It doesn't sound to me as though he's there to cause trouble."

"He was doing more than just making conversation, Walter. He was about to launch into a tirade. The king's enemy had a list of accusations to make against the men of the earth."

"But you didn't write that."

"Walter, good writers don't dump all the facts at one time. They conceal and then reveal at just the right time. They give you enough information to keep you thinking. A good writer brings you to certain conclusions slowly based on the plotline."

"Well, the only thing I see is a man tossing a snake into a hamster cage to see how they get along."

The Playwright sat back and stroked his long beard before responding.

"Walter, you're not thinking deeply enough. The undercurrents of life dwell in deep places that are only uncovered by such a tale. There is a rolling tide of evil that can only be stemmed by what is to be learned from this story. This man's life will be meaningful in the end."

"Take that as you may, I have further issues with the script."

"Go on."

"For example, the climax of the story occurs in the opening scenes. No rising action. No opportunity for the performers to voice startling revelations? The plot never develops. You don't even have a plot twist."

"Walter, what makes you think the climax is in the opening two scenes?"

"Well, let's see. Upon hearing the bad news, that you shovel onto the hero, he shaves his head, tears his clothes, and sits down in a pile of ashes. Sounds a little climactic to me."

"You are limiting the value of the man's life to what he possesses in this life and his relationships on earth. What if there is something more significant than the tangible elements of his life that I want to display for all the world to see?"

"Is it worth what he has to pay to become some trophy in your showcase? And then you have him spout out that ridiculous statement. "I was born naked, and I will die naked. The King gave me life and the king has taken it away. I will still bless him."

The Director smiles, choosing to ignore Walter's mocking fashion. "Oh, I love that line. It's one of my favorites."

"Really? Well, it's totally unrealistic. Who says stuff like that after they've had everything taken away from them?"

"People who trust the King."

Walter takes a step back as his eyes flash toward the Director.

"After that same King has unleashed the wrath of hell?"

"Especially after that."

Blind trust thought Walter. *The poppycock of fools and children. The opium of the spiritual masses. Only fools roll over and play dead when confronted with irrational statements.* Intellectual suicide was not his cup of tea.

Refusing to reveal his true feelings, Walter forced his face to play along.

"So, let me get this straight; to deepen the man's faith, the King invites his enemy into the throne room of heaven a second time to joust. As a result of that conversation, the man, who has lost everything, is now covered with boils and sores. Lovely. Sounds like a great story to read my children at bedtime."

"The King didn't exactly invite his enemy into his throne room."

"But he came. I mean, he was allowed in."

"Yes, and I asked him…"

"Where have you been," interrupted Walter. "Second verse same as the first, a lot, lot louder, and a lot, lot worse," he snarled. "You could've been a little more original in your writing. Then, instead of moving onto a new topic, the King brings up the man in the desert."

"I commend you, Walter. You certainly have read my script. Do you recall the enemy's challenge? 'A man will give anything to keep his life. But touch his body and he will curse you to your face.'"

"That's real world stuff, Walter."

Walter throws his hands in the air.

"There you have it! You release the rattlesnake of the cosmos on this poor defenseless man. From the soul of his foot to the crown of his head, pus flowed like a meandering stream. I would not have done that to my worst enemy. While we are on the topic, what about your other plays?"

"Such as?"

"*The Drowning of the Egyptian Army. An Ark for the Storm. Samson Brings the House Down.* And your blockbuster, *Brimstone and Fire on the Twin Cities.* Innocent people died!"

Walter noticed a change in the Director's demeanor. The anger he expected was strangely absent. His criticism of the Playwright's script was relentless, and yet, not an ounce of aggravation could be spotted in the Playwright's face. Instead, the Director's eyes softened and became moist. His voice cracked.

"He is neither poor nor defenseless. In fact, the man you pity was filled with power and garrisoned in with an army of protection."

"Well, somehow the protection broke down. The army abandoned him. What I see is a broken man, lying in the ashes, scraping his sores with pieces of pottery. Where's the power in that?"

Walter hears footsteps behind him. He turns to see the lead actor stepping out of the shadows. Walking to the apron of the stage the man speaks with a low and steady of voice."

"Shall we perform the closing narrative of Scene Two? Perhaps this will help him understand."

The Director nodded.

Instantly a woman storms in from stage left, almost knocking the lead to the ground.

"Do you still hold on to your honor? Why don't you curse the King and die," she cries out, with venom pouring out of every word.

"You talk like a women who has lost her mind. The King has been good to me. Why shouldn't I have to endure trouble from him?"

The lead and his wife drop their heads and exit stage right.

Walter folds his arms, digging his heels into the stage.

"And that is supposed to make sense to me? That somehow, because the King has been good to his royal subject, he now wins the right to inflict injury and loss. And why wasn't his wife taken out with the rest of his family?"

"You'll have to ask the villain, but I think the answer is quite obvious," replied the Playwright.

"I guess it pays to be mean," replied Walter.

"I wouldn't say she was mean, just had a bad moment."

"Oh, now you're being gracious?"

"Walter, I have a question for you."

"Go on."

"What do you think of his three friends who came to give him counsel after he was afflicted?"

"Oh, now I love those guys. You talk about the three amigos; those fellows are the best. Pointing their bony fingers in his face and setting him straight. What they share are gems of wisdom, priceless pearls of insight. Finally, someone in the story is using their heads."

"But what about their hearts," asked the Playwright.

"What do you mean?"

"There is very little compassion from these men. When a man or woman is suffering perhaps the best thing you can do is be very quiet and listen. They talked too much about things they didn't understand."

"And if they had listened, what would they had heard? 'Though he kills me, I will still trust him?' That is a fatalistic statement if I ever heard one," Walter rebuffed.

"No. They would have heard hope, faith and love. They would have heard one of the greatest statements ever to roll off the lips of a man."

"Which is?"

"I know my Redeemer lives, and I will stand before him when my life is over."

"I'm really confused. You destroy this man's life to bring him to a point where he declares an expectation of something he cannot hold in his hands or taste with his tongue?"

"I did not destroy his life; I cleansed it and purified it. I gave him new eyes for a greater vision than he had ever known. You see Walter, although he was a good man, the things of this world had become too important to him. He needed to be free so that he could truly enjoy all that the King of heaven had given him. The man also needed to be reminded that everything in this life of true value will be redeemed in the next."

"The Redeemer, that's it."

The Director smiled.

"The King who is ever present in every situation of life. There is nothing that he does not see. There is not a man or woman on the stage of life that he does not love and care about. The King is the true protagonist, the hero of my tale."

The Director gets up from his chair and begins to walk toward the stage. Tears stream down Walter's face.

"Your struggle is not with the story, is it?"

Walter slowly shook his head.

"I know your wife is dying of cancer."

Suddenly, Walter raises his head in anger and shouts through his tears at the approaching Playwright.

"And where was the King of heaven when she needed him?"

"He's been with her every step of the way. He never left her side. He also knows you're hurting, and he loves you very much. I know it's been difficult to be a part of this production, but I want you to know that the thunderous applause after the closing scene, somehow helps in the healing process. The King is not asking you to understand. In the end, all will be made whole, and you are here for a purpose. Your dear wife has gone through this for a reason. There's a bigger story being told by what you both are going through. Walter, there is a King in heaven. That means all things will be brought back to perfect wholeness, and you will stand before that King with all tears completely wiped away."

Tempted to turn and run out of the building, Walter instead ran into the arms of the Playwright. After a few moments of sobbing, he pulled away from the Director.

"I'm still angry," said Walter.

"I know. I don't blame you. What I have written is difficult."

The Playwright looked deeply into Walter's eyes, and placing his hands firmly on his shoulders, spoke in tenderness.

"Walter, I also want you to know that when your baby John died, I was right there to take him home. His little heart never developed but in heaven he runs free. He is held by arms that will never let him go. You'll see him soon."

"Hopefully not too soon."

They both laughed.

"I do like the ending though," said Walter, with a hint of a smile.

"How so?"

"You know, where you double everything that the man in the desert had before he lost it all. All except his children. He had seven before that day, and then, he had seven more. I hate to be picky but that doesn't add up to 14."

"Walter, the children were never lost to him. They were only separated from him for a short time. I did double his children."

"Alright, alright, but I love the way you chastise the man's wife for her disparaging comment."

"What do you mean?"

"Well, she had to give birth seven more times."

The Playwright only smiled.

"Can we resume our story now, Walter?"

"Yes, I'm ready to deliver my one line."

Returning to his chair, the Director raises his hand.

"Alright, everyone in their place. Let's not have the camels walk across the stage again. That was too stressful. Job, are you ready?"

"Yes."

"Action!"

CHAPTER 10

The Hero and the villain

Redemption is at the heart of one of our most beloved children's tales, brought to our generation courtesy of the Grimm brothers. The story of Snow White and the Seven Dwarfs laid buried in German folklore until Jacob and Wilhelm collected and published it, along with many other stories, in a book titled, *Grimms' Fairy Tales*.

The plot of the story is complicated, and winding, but it all boils down to a wicked queen, who is so self-absorbed with her own appearance that she becomes jealous of the beauty of a young maiden named Snow White. The evil queen is rebuffed by her magical mirror's declaration that Snow White is truly the fairest of them all. After several attempts to take her rival's life, the queen disguises herself as a witch and offers Snow White a poison apple. Falling into a deep sleep, she can only be revived by the kiss of a handsome prince. Love's true kiss brings her back from the horrors of an eternal slumber at the delight of the seven dwarfs.

This charming tale speaks volumes of what is at the heart and core of our shared human experience. Our ancient ancestors bit a poison apple and, as a result, we all slumber in a gray haze until awakened by one great act of redeeming love. Evil is then defeated and eternal good prevails. As this great struggle unfolded, two opposing forces appeared in the spotlight.

Behold, the hero. He is the knight in shining armor who saves the day by slaying the fire-breathing dragon. She is the young girl who can shoot an arrow through the heart of a rabbit at one hundred yards and then use that same weapon to deliver her oppressed people. The hero is the cowboy who can rescue a prairie township from the bad guys by reluctantly pinning on a tin star. We sit in the theater and wait for the appearance of the one who will deliver the goods and rescue the moment. Our fingers flip through the pages of a novel to reach the instant of the conquering hero's pointed blade. We love to rout for the protagonist.

Behold, the villain. The purveyor of evil schemes set forth to entangle the plot and destroy any hope of a happy ending. Sometimes hidden from view, they reveal themselves midstory, and we quickly love to hate them. The wicked witch of the west swings her broom and releases her terrifying flying monkeys to block the way to Oz. Sweeney Todd and Mrs. Lovett pair up to provide us with a bone-chilling experience. Todd, the "demon barber of Fleet Street," cuts throats with a shave a bit too close while Mrs. Lovett turns their corpses into meat pies. Miss Trunchbull sings, "The Smell of Rebellion," as a salute to her hatred of children. Fortunately, Matilda fared much better than the chubby little boy who ate the entire chocolate cake. We long for the villain's downfall. We patiently wait for the hero's victory.

As a small boy growing up in simpler times, the weekends had a definite pattern. Saturday mornings were filled with Bugs Bunny and the Road Runner while the afternoon gave way to Audie Murphy and Chuck Connor as *The Rifleman*. It was easy to spot the hero and to know that in the end he or she would triumph. In those days, the villain would step out from behind a thorny bush with a twisted face. The good guy would always wear white as he rode off into the sunset. The bad guy wore black and met his just end either in death or defeat. Even their names revealed the wholesomeness or poison of their character. When Dudley Do-right was on the trail of Snidely Whiplash, no one had to wonder who the hero was versus the villain.

These common storylines were not created in a vacuum. Their roots were buried in the soil of an age, long ago. In fact, the very first hero and villain story was played out in a theater beyond our reach or full understanding. It all began long before man appeared on the world's stage. The origins of theater drama started with an evil character who shocked the courts of heaven with a brazen attempt at mutiny. The story will end with his total defeat by the hands of a righteous conqueror. Subsequently, the wicked antagonist in fierce divergence against the righteous protagonist is at the root of all stage productions. The wounded hero peers into the face of his archenemy as he slowly pulls the arrow out of his shoulder. Tossing it to the ground, they stand toe to toe. It is a story older than time, and yet, as new as the latest Broadway hit. Let us first introduce and then contrast these two main characters.

God, eternal in the heavens, is the hero of redemption's story. Dwelling in light unapproachable, he is ablaze with the glory of his righteousness. His holiness brings health and wholeness to all of creation. His power is without measure, his knowledge knows no bounds, and his presence fills every corner of creation. He is worthy of worship and adoration from angels and men alike.

Lucifer, the mighty archangel and leader of the choir of heaven, was beautiful in his appearance. Yielding powerful influence among his fellow angels, he was given freedom to use his creativity in service to his Creator. Lucifer was described as the morning star, bright and glorious. He was the chief angel until he attacked the Creator. Lucifer led a white-fisted rebellion with a group of fellow angels, desiring to sit on God's throne. Now, the difference between the two could not be more obvious.

Lucifer became Satan, meaning the adversary. The "son of the morning," now prefers lurking in the shadows while keeping his identity unknown. He uses misinformation and lies concerning God's character and intent. After man's fall in the garden, Satan uses the smokescreen of deception. He is also called the devil, meaning the slanderer or accuser in direct reference to his evil finger-pointing at the children of God. He propagates the glorification of man over his Creator. He whispers the falsehood that man is the center of the universe. Satan spreads the lie that the problem of mankind is not one of sin, but of the circumstances that surround him. This leads man to believe that he alone determines his destiny, all the while being led to the very door of hell by his rebellion against a loving, merciful God. The Director's kindness and patience are viewed as weakness. All of this is done in a smoke-filled environment, wherein Satan is reduced to a red cape with horns and a tail. The Devil does his best work in the dark, causing mankind to see him as nothing more than a comic strip character.

In contrast, God works in the light because he is light. He hides nothing from mankind that would advance him for good. His beauty is seen all around us and his love is shown through his healing and transformation of people. The world is warmed by the sun and comforted through nature. Through the ages God has revealed himself by sending prophets and sages to communicate his love. He sent his angels to warn Sodom and Gomorrah and Jonah to preach to Nineveh. In the ultimate expression of his love, he sent his only son, Jesus, to die in our place to bring us back to God. He has given us the book of Revelation to warn us of the end times and flee from the wrath to come. In our day, the majority of pulpits are filled with good men attempting to point people to heaven. He has been nothing but benevolent and kind.

Unfortunately, the Devil has cast a gray haze over the eyes of men. As a result, the hero and the villain are not always easy to discern. God is viewed as distant and uncaring while Satan is portrayed as cartoonish. The great lie, that God was holding back Adam and Eve's true liberty in the Garden of Eden, is still whispered today. The truth that he sent his only begotten Son, for the most part, falls on deaf ears. Jesus, God's champion, is seen as a good teacher but nothing more. His life is considered weak and his death on the cross only bolsters their assessment. His return as the Lion of Judah is considered folklore. The question of hero and villain is the great struggle of the human heart.

To further muddy the waters, Satan offers a pseudo liberty through the bait of worldly power and wealth. The dangling carrot of happiness is kept just out of reach as the devil delights to see mankind reaching out for his empty promises. Satan gives just enough satisfaction to keep men quietly on the path to hell. Wide is the way that leads to destruction, and narrow is the road that leads to life.

In the opening scene of this epic battle, Lucifer attempted to overthrow the King of heaven by placing his throne above the "Most High." The theme of the book of Revelation is whether God and his Son, Jesus Christ will rule or will Satan and his followers ultimately win the day. The matter was settled at the cross, but until that victory plays out, the battle rages on. The days of our lives pass with quiet reminders of this intense, personal struggle reflected in our own internal fight between good and evil. This truth is embedded within us because it flows from the taproot of that first conflict. And so, we create heroes and rogues.

Consider the following examples… George Bailey squares off against Potter for the control of the Bailey Business and Loan. Hamlet, the Prince of Denmark, seeks revenge on King Claudius for the murder of his father. In some stories, the antagonist is not a person but an entity such as in, *To Kill a Mockingbird*. Atticus Finch, the hero, battles the villain of the social expectations of Maycomb, Alabama. In the struggle to set God's people free, Moses reenters the land of his birth to defy the Pharoah of Egypt with nothing more than a staff and his faith in God. Evil and good must be personified because the struggle between God and Lucifer was, and still is, personal. Therefore, Satan's move to subvert his Creator can only be described by the word, mutiny.

In his book, *The Wager*, David Grann describes the essence of mutiny as it occurred on the HMS Wager in 1741. The captain of the Wager, David Cheap, was left to die on a storm-blown island by members of his own crew. Grann writes, "A full-blown mutiny was unlike other revolts. It took place within the very forces, established by the state to impose order —the military— which is why it was so often brutally squashed."[114] He continues, "This is why mutinies capture the public imagination. What was it that drove the enforcement of order to descend into disorder?"[115]

In my book, *The Seventh Trail, Journey to the Well of Chayah*, I attempt to describe the rebellion of Lucifer through a fictional story told by a demon named Boar. The tale is told from the twisted, demonic perspective of Boar himself. In his willowing, twisted voice, the demon skews the truth of what actually happened on the day his master rebelled. God is portrayed as a jealous deity, and Lucifer is viewed as the offended party. This is the story of the day of the Bright Light…

"We sang to the heavens, for we were the Chief Chorus, able to reach notes and blend harmonies beyond imagination. Songs poured out of us with such explosive creativity that no melody was ever sung twice. Our music sprang forth like fresh fountains of water, ever new, refreshing all who listened. Our beauty knew no bounds; our glory was unsurpassed. Our leader, Moraw (Lucifer), led us to higher and higher ground, until one day everything changed. Our leader had excelled to heights that caused the Evil One (God) to grow jealous. The beauty and power of Moraw threatened him in a way we did not understand. On the day of the Bright Light, when the Evil One could no longer contain his jealousy, he stormed into the throne room. Moraw sat high above us, leading us in the worship of himself. As our voices trailed off in disbelief, the Evil One ascended the throne and challenged Moraw to battle. It was then we saw the Bright Light."[116]

"Lucifer's pride resulted in the introduction of sin into God's created order. With his fall from the heights, the Shining One became the Angel of Darkness, and the host of angels that followed him became demons. His glory was gone, and his brilliance turned to eternal gloom. He may present himself as an angel of light, but his true reality is darkness. By the act of his free will, the mighty archangel chose to become Satan, which means, an adversary. By this one inconceivable act, Lucifer, and those who followed him, became unredeemable agents of doom, destined for eternal punishment."[117]

To make matters worse, Satan's rebellion included one third of the angels resulting in their immediate expulsion from the celestial realm. Along with their leader they became demonic spirits reserved for the fires of hell. However, the eternal flames of punishment were not sufficient to rid God's creation from the poison of his enemy. Something more was required to reinstate holiness and wholeness. Lucifer was part of God's created order. He was connected with the earth, and thus, God decreed that someone from the earth had to conquer him. This alone would restore the terrestrial domain to righteousness. God placed the responsibility of vanquishing his foe in the hands of an unlikely combatant.

Strange as it must sound, the Director of heaven brings out his warrior in the mixture of clay and spirit. He decided to destroy the works of the Devil through his greatest creation, mankind, and he did this for a very specific reason. Lucifer, having been cast down to the earth, had assumed a quasi-control of what belonged to God. Exerting an authority he did not have; Satan claimed a dominion he believed he deserved. God's command that man should have dominion over creation was a direct challenge to Satan. Before we examine how this grand experiment played out, we must digress.

When Lucifer's rebellion occurred, man had not yet been created. To this day, the Devil is not angry with man nor God's creation. His desire remains the same as in the day of his white-fisted challenge to deity. His aspiration to subvert the throne of heaven and capture God's glory stills burns in his heart. Satan's continued attack against mankind is an attempt to injure God, not man. The world is collateral damage in a battle that has raged for longer than we have existed. Subsequently, man is nothing more than a means to an end, a pawn in Satan's chess game. Mankind was created for God's glory and to release Satan's hold on the created order. The Devil's goal is to thwart his enemy's plan by blinding mankind. "In their case the god of this world has blinded the minds of the unbelievers, to keep them from seeing the light of the gospel of the glory of Christ, who is the image of God."[118]

To draw first blood, Satan immediately attacked Adam and Eve. By entering paradise, he disturbed their tranquility and shattered the simplicity of their walk with God. He appeared as a beautiful serpent to offer the temptation of supposed freedom. He questioned God's goodness by implying that he was holding something back from Eve. Like pieces on a board game, Satan moved to claim God's greatest creation as his own possession. Pulling Eve into his web of deceit, he attempted to deny them both their rightful place of dominion over God's creation. However, Satan's presence in the garden raises difficulties.

From a logical standpoint, it is reasonable to question this scene. Why was Satan allowed access to the garden? The first couple appeared frail in comparison to one so mighty as the Devil. It feels like an overreach to expect Eve to resist. God could have easily barred his entrance or at least given his first couple some time to grow in their walk with him. Still, we must not fall into the trap of seeing Adam and Eve as we understand mankind now.

When first created, Adam and Eve were magnificent in every way. They were physical and mental specimens in a form so far above our present view. It would amaze us to see their abilities in every sphere of human life. Speaking of man, "You made him for a little while lower than the angels; you have crowned him with glory and honor."[119] Adam and Eve were fresh from being hand-crafted by God and had not been tainted by sin. They were well equipped to takeover God's creation and conquer the Lord's enemy.

However, the path soon turned dark. With one fatal choice, Adam and Eve cast aside their glorious future and ran for cover. Before entering this maze of mystery, a few things need to be considered from a theoretical standpoint.

Firstly, one might think that God would have destroyed his enemy simply uttering the word. As the old saying goes, "I brought you into this world and I can take you out!" Along that line of reasoning God would have prevented Satan's entrance into the garden in the form of a serpent. That act alone would have cleared the way for mankind to enjoy his Creator without the danger of a temptation. It makes perfect sense to surround those whom you love with the covering of protection. However, the Director makes no mistakes, so he must have had a reason for allowing Satan into paradise.

Adam and Eve were created in a state of innocence. It was God's plan to test them in order for innocence to become holiness. Holiness could not be given; it had to be attained by obedience in the midst of a trial. Adam and Eve were on probation with one great test to pass. If our ancestors would have obeyed God and not eaten of the forbidden fruit, then access to the tree of life would be granted. Their natural lives would have been transformed into spiritual lives, and they would have lived forever in their physical bodies. Let us reason further.

God had created an eternal being in Lucifer, and through him, sin had entered creation. Eternal damnation in a lake of fire was decreed as Satan's punishment, but first, he must be cast out of the creation which he had polluted. By the obedience of that one test in the garden, Adam and Eve were to be the warriors who defeated him. Obviously, that did not happen.

When Adam and Eve sinned, all their descendants and creation became collateral damage. The apple doesn't fall far from the tree as the generations that proceeded down from that first couple have testified. We have produced a world of sinners. The depravity of fallen man has reached limits in these last days that are shocking. Adam and Eve utterly failed to achieve dominion, and we have been flopping on the shore like fish out of water ever since. But God's purposes can never be frustrated, and so, Satan's ultimate defeat would have to come from a plot twist that no one saw coming.

When all seemed lost, God's protagonist arrived on the scene. Born in the humblest conditions, and yet a true hero, Jesus Christ came as one of us. He was the most unlikely protagonist.

The Lion, the Witch, and the Wardrobe is a classic children's tale with heavy overtones of redemption complete with hero and villain alike. C. S. Lewis develops characters such as Aslan and the White Witch to help us understand the great story of rescue from the darkness that fills the human heart. Jay Rudd writes, "In chapter 13 of *The Lion, the Witch, and the Wardrobe*, titled, 'Deep Magic from the Dawn of Time," the lion Aslan volunteers himself as a substitute for Edmond, whose life has been forfeited to the White Witch according to the deep magic written on the Table of Stone. The Witch herself encourages Aslan to articulate the law.[120] Lewis writes, "You at least know the magic which the Emperor put into Narnia at the very beginning. You know that every traitor belongs to me as my lawful prey and that for every treachery I have a right to kill."[121]

Edmund has committed betrayal in Narnia and deserves death. Both Aslan and the White Witch are quite clear on this point. The symbolism is stunning. Adam and Eve forfeited their right to gain dominion and rule. The "deep magic," pictures God's eternal decree that sin must be punished by death.

Rudd continues… "There seems to be no way out of the dilemma. Even Aslan seems powerless to stop the execution."[122] Again, as the Witch puts it, "do you really think your master can rob me of my rights by mere force? He knows the deep magic better than that. He knows that unless I have blood as the Law says all Nadia will be overturned and perish in fire and water."[123] Clearly, blood must be spilt to satisfy the Emperor's Deep Magic, and the only way to save Edmond is for Aslan to volunteer his own life in exchange."[124]

The Hero of heaven, Jesus Christ, gave his life on a cruel cross to pay for the sins of all mankind. Lewis's symbolism could not be more riveting. However, this unexpected turn in the story was ordain long before the events of the crucifixion. In fact, his mission to rescue the sons of men from the darkened stage of sin was in process before the dawn of time and foretold before Jesus walked the earth. "Knowing that you were ransomed from the futile ways inherited from your forefathers, not with perishable things such as silver or gold, but with the precious blood of Christ, like that of a lamb without blemish or spot. He was foreknown before the foundation of the world but was made manifest in the last times for the sake of you."[125] There was a moment in the life of Abraham that he recognized God by a very specific name. By using that name, he acknowledged that the Sovereign of the universe had always had designs for his life and was never caught off guard.

Abraham and Sarah had finally received the promised son, Isaac. He was a young boy when God told Abraham to take him to Mount Moriah to sacrifice him. As they climbed the hill together Isaac asked his father, "Behold, the fire and the wood, but where is the lamb for a burnt offering?"[126] His father responded that the LORD would provide the lamb. As Abraham raised the knife to kill his son God stopped him just in time. Relieved, he looked up to see a ram caught in a thicket. That day, Abraham called God, Jehovah Jireh, which means, "the one who provides."

Long before the first dew of creation's morn, God had already set in motion a plan to rescue us. Jesus, God's only son, went to a cross, but unlike Isaac, he was not spared death. He alone is the Hero on heaven's stage. In his death and resurrection, he has conquered the villain, Satan.

However, the story continues to develop. His victory has become our triumph over the darkness of sin. "Nay, in all these things we are more than conquerors through him that loved us."[127]

When Joshua was leading the conquest for the land of Canaan, he came into conflict with the five kings of the Amorites. After routing the enemy and commanding the sun to stand still, Joshua learned that the five kings were hiding in a cave. He immediately commanded a stone to be rolled over the entrance to trap these cowardly rulers. His plan was to reveal the essence of our victory over God's enemy.

"And when they brought those kings out to Joshua, Joshua summoned all the men of Israel and said to the chiefs of the men of war who had gone with him, "Come near; put your feet on the necks of these kings." Then they came near and put their feet on their necks."[128] But he wasn't finished. "And Joshua said to them, "Do not be afraid or dismayed; be strong and courageous. For thus the LORD will do to all your enemies against whom you fight."[129]

There is no struggle or battle for the followers of Jehovah. By faith in his completed work, we simply place our foot on the neck of sin. The fight is the Lords', and he is already victorious. We march forward from a *place* of victory, not in order to achieve it.

Our discussion of the Hero and a Villain leads us to one great question. Which side you will choose? We are all active participants in the great battle between good and evil, between right and wrong, whether we know it or not. Charles Dickens, in his classic novel, *David Copperfield*, begins by posing this question by the story's hero, "*I am born.* Whether I shall turn out to be the hero of my own story, or whether that station will be held by anybody else, these pages must show."[130]

The choice ought to be obvious to all of us, but that theory is rebuffed by the words of Jesus. "Enter by the narrow gate. For the gate is wide and the way is easy that leads to destruction, and those who enter by it are many. For the gate is narrow and the way is hard that leads to life, and those who find it are few."[131] We are all in the midst of the battle and must decide which banner we will march under. We are so much more than simply pawns on a chessboard. Mary McCarthy was wrong when she wrote, "We all live in suspense from day to day; in other words, you are the hero of our own story."[132]

Jesus is the great protagonist who has conquered the enemy of our souls and become our hero. His victory *is* our victory. In his strength we place our feet on our enemy's neck. The second Adam has prevailed where the first Adam failed, and as a matter of course, we now may eat of the Tree of Life and gain the dominion lost to us in the garden. "For sin will have no dominion over you, since you are not under law but under grace."[133]

He is the hero of our story, and we live in the 'station' of triumph as a result of being born again.

CHAPTER 11

Comedy club

I t is a world filled with savagery played out in an arena where men are shredded to pieces and women are drawn and quartered. Few survive this darkened hall of agony, and for those who wander back into the light, their remaining days are filled with the haunting memories of silent audiences, or worse, abusive hecklers. The smell of tar and a covering of feathers is not easily forgotten. These unfortunate souls, these tortured beings, are the reckless few who have attempted to walk onto a stage in a comedy club, and brutal does not begin to describe their experience.

Good comedy is a tough act and few there are who can beat the drum well. First experiences are enough to scare most of these brave souls into early retirement. Their day jobs are instantly more appealing. If they do continue to walk down that slippery slope, the mounting pressure to write new and better monologues drive most to take up banging their heads against a wall for a past time. We might be tempted to pity these poor folks with their self-inflicted wounds, but it is important to remember they are willing participates in this blood sport.

Perhaps you have never thought of it, but comedy serves an important role. The weaving of humor into life carries with it a very specific purpose. The men and women who travel the clown circuit are trying to accomplish a noble feat. These martyrs of mirth, with all their flops and fumbles, are really trying to help us. Jokesters unite! Your efforts are not in vain; your bravery and sacrifice are not unappreciated. We need your services.

A healthy life involves balance. The weights and counterweights of any given day keep us fully functioning. Inactivity fills us with nervous energy and growing anxiety. However, an inordinate amount of activity or drama turns us into a frazzled, tired mess. In the orchestra pit, strings that are never loosened will eventually break. A family or community under constant duress will not long endure. Humor is the equalizer to the pressures of life, and not surprisingly, it is the invention of the Playwright.

In, *The Play That Goes Wrong*, nothing goes right. Written by Lewis, Sayer, and Shields, it is a British farce produced by the Mischief Theater Company of London. From start to finish, a play that should have been a classic whodunit, turns into a series of comedic errors unforeseen by the serious actors and actresses who desperately want to solve the mystery of who killed Charles Haversham. Props misfire, lines can't be remembered, and murder victims won't stay dead. The play connects with the audience because it resembles life. That is why the script so funny. We want life to run like a clock, but most of time, the clock goes cuckoo. The second hand slows, and the springs break until we sit down with no other option but to laugh.

I grew up in a farmhouse in the country. I can still go back in my mind and walk through our house on the hill. The staircase and the bedrooms upstairs are fixed in my memory. Sitting on the couch in our living room I faced the old Zenith with its four channels. Passing through the dining room, I can still see my seat at the oval shaped table. Walking through a doorway into our narrow kitchen, I can see our small fridge and limited countertop. On the stove sat a large metal pot with a valve sitting on top. That old pewter crock would begin to rumble and shake causing all kinds of ruckus. Finally, the pressure was too much, and it exploded with a steady flow of hot steam from its small valve. The ham that sat inside didn't have a chance. I always waited for an explosion from that pressure cooker, but it never came thanks to a small valve sitting on the lid.

Laughter is like that valve; it gives us relief from the pressures of life. As a twelve-year-old boy I read a narrative at a Christmas program at church. I warned my mother repeatedly that my nerves would cause me to laugh. She should have listened. Once we discover the humor hidden, which invariably lies within most situations, the difficulty eases and we can face life anew.

Now, some people are born with a sense of humor and others take a more serious tone. The first group look for the funny stuff in every situation. They point out the absurd as they poke us in the side. The second group reminds us to stay on the task at hand. We need both. If everyone was a clown, there would be no targeted audience. If there was no one who got aggravated because we moved their stapler, where is the fun in that. Likewise, the serious remind us there are times not to poke the funny bone. For both crowds, comedy is essential to a healthy life. Ecclesiastes tells us that there is a time to laugh.[134] Always be ready to laugh even in the midst of difficulty.

As Erma Bombeck, a famous columnist for over thirty years once wrote, "There is a thin line that separates laughter from pain, comedy from tragedy, humor and hurt."[135] The ability to laugh in the midst of hardship is a gift from the hand of God. There are also health benefits. Those who study such things tell us that a good hardy laugh reduces our stress levels and causes our muscles to relax for up to 45 minutes. Like that pressure valve on my mother's cooker, laughter keeps us from exploding. In times of high suspense what is desperately needed is a good old fashion belly laugh. Researchers at Mayo Clinic conclude, "Laughter enhances your intake of oxygen-rich air, stimulates your heart, lungs and muscles, and increases the endorphins that are released by your brain."[136]

Humor also boosts our immune system. "Negative thoughts manifest into chemical reactions that can affect your body by bringing more stress into your system and decreasing your immunity. By contrast, positive thoughts can actually release neuropeptides that help fight stress and potentially more-serious illnesses."[137]

Long before these reports came out, the Bible agreed, "A joyful heart is good medicine, but a crushed spirit dries up the bones."[138] Clearly, our mental condition affects our physical being. Even Job's miserable counselors spoke wisdom at times. Bildad told his broken friend, lying in the ashes, "He will yet fill your mouth with laughter and your lips with shouting."[139] The Bible is full of sidesplitting moments.

In a pathetically hilarious scene, King Nebuchadnezzar of Babylon set up a band in the desert with strange instruments to prompt worship to an image he had built of himself. The vanity of powerful people is a common trait. As the King struck up the band, he insisted that, Shadrach, Meshach, and Abednego, three Jewish captives, fall and worship the statue. True to their devotion to Jehovah the three men refused. Knowing that their punishment was a fiery furnace they remained with locked knees with their eyes fixed on heaven. The King was furious. The heavenly audience sat with bated breath as Nebuchadnezzar ordered the furnace to be stroked seven times hotter than usual. At his order, the guards grabbed the three unrepented warriors and threw them into the flames.

At this point, everyone headed for the exits concluding that the antagonist had won the day. But this is where the fun began. Nebuchadnezzar ran to a small window in the furnace and was astonished to see four men walking in the fire. He questioned the guards, "Didn't you throw three men in the furnace?" They had indeed, but the King saw four men in the fire and the fourth appeared as an angel. In a paradigm shift that would make your head spin, the King proclaimed that the God of Shadrach, Meshach, and Abednego was the true God.

Shadrach Meshach, and Abednego proved their metal by choosing the furnace rather than being unfaithful to their God. As they stepped into the flames their feet never felt so cool. The three men were fireproof. Not a hair on their chinny chin chin was singed. They also enjoyed the added benefit of dancing the jig with a fourth man in the furnace, who was none other than the Lord himself. In the end, the only thing the fire destroyed were the cords that bound their hands and feet. The circumstances that led up to this moment were beyond their control, but what they could control was their faithfulness to the Playwright.

Finally, the joke was on the foolish King. He had no other choice but to confess that the statue he had created was powerless. The three Jewish slaves were the stars of the show. Under the Director's watchful eye, we are the freest when we are in the hottest water, or the fiery furnace. The idols of men are torn down, and the band goes home sad when the Director of heaven shows up. If the story's not good, the story's not over.

As a little boy I possessed an insatiable hunger for being mischievous. In our house on North Grand my bedroom was above the living room where my father would sit watching television. An iron register lay in the floor just above his chair. For you young whippersnappers a register is a hole in the floor with a grate over it. Its purpose is to allow the heat to be transferred to the upstairs. My father's chair was directly below the register. Each night, while watching television, my dad would sit with a tub of ice cream in his lap. My brother and I, who were supposed to be sleeping, would kneel over top of the register and watch our father. Finished with his ice cream he would lean back and fall into a deep sleep. Lee and I then tied a rubber spider to a string and dropped it onto his stomach. After the spider danced a jig we would draw it up and then redirect him over my father's open mouth. The goal was always to see how far down into his mouth we could drop the spider before he woke up. He would inevitably awake yelling for us to get in bed. These are good memories I still treasure today. In the tough times we think back and those moments of humor cheer us to press onward in life. Not surprisingly, the future King in Israel needed moments of hysterical theater.

David was on the run from King Saul. After nourishing himself with some holy bread from Ahimelech the priest, he took off for the pagan territory. David sought to seek protection from King Achish of Gath. However, his strategy quickly turned sour. The servants of Achish reminded him of a song recently sung in Israel concerning Saul and David. "And the women sang to one another as they celebrated, "Saul has struck down his thousands, and David his ten thousand."[140] Achish understood the jealousy that Saul might harbor, and he began to see David as a threat. Fear filled David's heart. He knew he had to do something quickly, and so, impromptu was the flavor of the day.

Having little time to think, David decided to feign madness. With his hands waving in the air, and spittle running down his beard, he danced and cried out until the King shook his head. Wild mushrooms must be a bumper crop in Israel this year, thought Achish. The King turned to his counselors and reminded them that there was no lack of nut cases in his own court, and the last thing he needed was one more at his table. David was removed from a dangerous situation because of his twisted funny bone. Walking away he had to smile to himself. As the droll hung from his whiskers he couldn't wait to get back home to embellish his sideshow. Goofing around with his older brothers had finally paid off.

In the mix of ministry, Jesus reminded his disciples of the need to unwind and blow off a little stream. His men had just returned from a wildly successful missionary endeavor. Demons had been cast out, the sick were healed, and lives were changed. The central message they preached was one of repentance. Rather than celebrate their successes, and launch them back out into the fray, Jesus saw the need to take the group in a different direction. He recognized that the weight of ministry was unsustainable, and so, he gave them a surprising command. "Come apart by yourselves to a desolate place and rest for a while."[141] They needed to unwind and recharge. As Vance Havner once said, "If you don't come apart, you *will* come apart."[142]

To enter the happiness of the Playwright of heaven is all the compensation we will need or desire. Our reward when we enter heaven is that we will enter the joy of our Lord. We will be free to laugh and be joyful in his presence. If happiness will be our lot in glory, should we not partake in it now? His presence now is no less real than it will be then, even in the battles we face.

Elijah was a mighty prophet whom God used in tense times. Even as Israel was drying up from a draught, the preacher's comedic spirit remained intact. His ability to use humor was on full display on top of Mt. Carmel. It had been three years since rain fell, and the ground was parched. Crops withered as herds of cattle and sheep were slowly dying. King Ahab sat on the throne of a country in dire straits of a good soaking. There was no joy in "Whoville."

Rather than blame himself, the King cast all the fault on Elijah for the failed crops and dying cattle. Think of it, Ahab had sinned, but it was the prophet who had a bounty on his head. In a world that has turned upside down this all makes good sense. Elijah sent a message to Ahab that he was willing to meet and discuss the present dilemma. Following a short and unproductive conversation, Elijah challenged the prophets of Baal to a contest on top of Mount Carmel.

As the sun rose the next morning, it was easy to see that Elijah was outnumbered. In one of the most spectacular displays of God's hand in the affairs of men, the crusty old preacher stood before 450 prophets of Baal with grit in his teeth and an attitude of a badger. The crowd was an audience of uncommitted Israelites. They would decide at the end of the day which way the wind blew, and based on that, make their decision. As Elijah took center stage, he laid down the rules of the contest.

An altar was built, a bull was slaughtered, but no fire was to be placed upon the altar. Both sides would have an opportunity to call down fire from heaven. The God who answered by fire was the true God. Elijah could have made short work of the clustered clowns of Baal, but he chose instead to entertain the crowd with a show they would never forget. The prophets of Baal would go first. Let the games begin, and may the odds be ever in the true prophet's favor.

From morning to noon, the disciples of Baal trumpeted, "O Baal, answer us." Awkwardness filled the hillside as silence fell upon the crowd. The gathering grew anxious and weary of the sham show. Rotten tomatoes began to fly. A chorus of boos ricocheted off the mountains cascading into the valleys. The bogus performance continued as the prophets limped around the altar in exhaustion. The call to Baal was to no avail.

Elijah smiled from his perch in a nearby sycamore tree. After finishing off his last fig, he hopped down and approached the assembly of religious charlatans. In a fine display of showmanship, he raised his hands and made several suggestions to aid the tired impostors.

Perhaps he stated, "You are not noisy enough. Since Baal is a god, he awaits a deeper display of your devotion," Elijah suggested. "Maybe he is busy thinking through some long math equation?" Then, turning to the crowd, "I know what the holdup is, he's sitting on the toilet, reading the funnies. Possibly he is sound asleep and refuses to be awakened." Now I know I have speculated a bit, but the entire scene smacks with comedy. Elijah had been bored by a brook for three years, and he was possibly a bit punchy. He was no doubt savoring the moment and registering it for his grandchildren.

Rather than admit defeat, the tired prophets intensified their efforts. They cried louder and cut themselves with swords and lances until the blood poured. They continued this foolish facade until the evening sacrifice. In response, the heavens took upon itself a stony silence. Impressive in performance, but empty in results would be the review written in the Jerusalem Times. In perfect timing and showmanship Elijah stepped forward.

With an economy of words, the true prophet of God called down fire from the heavens and consumed the altar but not before pouring gallons of water all over the dead bull. The crowd of people who had come to watch and decide were duly impressed.

When God is on a man's side, he always outnumbers the opposition. The Playwright's best lines are on the side of the one who trusts him so deeply that a leisurely approach can be enjoyed because the battle is the Lord's. The Playwright takes pleasure in the one who can smile and have a little fun at the expense of the posers. "He who sits in the heavens laughs; the Lord holds them in derision."[143] However, there is a deeper story involving humor in the Bible concerning a long-awaited son.

God arrived one day at the tent of Abraham to make an astounding announcement. He would have a son in his old age. Abraham fell down and laughed. Since he had long ago passed the time he could produce an heir, he just couldn't restrain himself. However, he was not laughing at God but at himself. This was the laughter of faith. Abraham finally understood that in his own strength, he could not bring to pass the promises of God. Our father of faith had reached a maturity in his walk with God wherein he fully trusted him. It was a good laugh. Unfortunately, Abraham's wife, Sarah, had a different response.

For many long and agonizing years, Sarai had traveled through life with no child to call her own. Hope had withered and died on the vine with each passing month. Regardless of the promise of God concerning a child, the last thing she expected was to be changing diapers. Her hope of giving birth had died with her womb, and it was a topic her husband no doubt avoided like a swarm of locusts. But when the three visitors showed up, she had to face the camel in the tent, and for her it was not a laughing matter.

After a hastily prepared meal the men sat in the shade of a large tree and spoke with Abraham about the future. As Sarah milled about the entrance of their tent, she overheard the men talking. What they said shocked her. About this time next year, they would have a child of their own. Unfortunately, Sarai's response was one of laughter.

Hidden behind the tent's canvas, her soft chuckle included a heavy dose of anger and frustration toward the Lord. Sarah scoffed at the prediction of these heavenly visitors, regarding it as idle chitchat. Regrettably, they heard her laugh. She had been caught in a moment of deep unbelief. Sarah's attempt to deny her mocking tone fell flat, and she stood guilty as charged. "Is anything too had for God," they asked.

Within months she was pregnant. Sarah's conception was a shock to both her and Abraham. Nine months later she sat in her tent, nursing her son. She began to laugh again, but this time it was different. Her laughter now was an expression of joy at the arrival of her newborn and an outburst of triumphant faith. She sent out birth announcements that read, "Come laugh with me." Appropriately, they named him Isaac, which means laughter.

Before we come to believe in Christ, we chuckle at the idea that a penniless carpenter from Nazareth can make any difference in our lives. With a quiet snicker we set him aside as irrelevant. The prophet Isaiah wrote, "He was despised and rejected by men, a man of sorrows and acquainted with grief; and as one from whom men hide their faces, he was despised, *and we esteemed him not.*" (Emphasis mine)[144] There is no use denying it, we have all weighed him in the balance and found him lacking. However, then came the great day when we bowed our knees to the One who died for us, and the mocking laughter turned to joyous laughter. This was the case with Sarah. Jesus is truly the one who brings us joy that erupts into a belly laugh. The comedy club of the Director is especially with those who are hurting because God always gets the last laugh.

Mephibosheth was the grandson of King Saul but that did little to help him. His life was a "series of unfortunate events." Few things went well for the young boy beginning with his ridiculously difficult name. Imagine trying to fit Mephibosheth into a theater program. Notwithstanding, his story began with a tragic event when he was just five years old. It was an early plot twist that would change his life, but in the end land him a place at the King's table. It all began with the bitter kiss of family death.

King Saul, his grandfather, was on his way out of power, and unfortunately, he was not exiting the stage gracefully. You might say the scene was changing, and he would not yield the floor. In fact, Saul attempted to kill his replacement, David, on several occasions. With a murderous spirit, Saul clung to his lead part. Jonathan, who was the King's son and father of Mephibosheth, maintained a close friendship with David.

After news arrived of both his father and grandfather's death in battle, the nurse of Mephibosheth took the young boy and fled. As they raced to safety, the lad fell and became lame in both of his feet. Now crippled, the future seemed bleak for the little fellow who had been born into a royal family. Shall we say, "More soup please."

The boy was hidden away for years until David came to the throne. The King asked, "Is there still anyone left of the house of Saul, that I may show him kindness for Jonathan's sake?"[145] The inquiry drew the young man before the King, and grace was extended. Mephibosheth was given all the wealth his family still possessed and a seat at the royal table till his dying day. His story went from a promising future to a tragic fall, and then, blessings under the favor of King David. As he sat at the table, his crippled legs were covered, and Mephibosheth sat as tall as any man.

We look for sunny days while God gives us rainbows after the passing storm. We imagine we've reached the end of the road until we see a detour leading to a brighter future. In the end he laughs with us as he showers us with blessings.

God has a sense of humor like no other. He perfectly understands its timing and freely uses it when needed. We rarely think of comedy as a part of God's character, and yet, laughter fills the story of redemption.

My friend, Mary, is a professional comedian. Her weekly joke to our Seniors' class at church lightens the spirits of those in attendance. She sends us out laughing. We need stand-up comedians. The last thing we want is for them to sit down and be quiet. The benefits received from the people who make us laugh is enormous. They may struggle at times to get the timing of a joke just right but give them grace. We carry our burdens and comedians knock on the door bidding us to get some fresh air. They are helping us to escape reality for a little while, and the reprieve is desperately needed.

However, there is coming a time on heaven's stage that comedy will take on a new light and a new purpose. In the not-so-distant future the Director will call the cast home and will wipe all tears from their eyes. We will no longer carry the burdens and heartaches of this life, and so, there will be no need to escape through comedy. Humor will still be a part of the performance in heaven but in a new way. The back slapping will continue, but humor's purpose will be transformed. Comedy will be used for the pure joy of its expression. Perhaps we should think of heaven as one long, continuous belly laugh. No longer as a means of escape from the heaviness of life, it will be for the simple fun of it all. In the end, we may finally understand why the chicken crossed the road.

CHAPTER 12

Blocking and body language

R hett Butler's smile was both charming and sinister. As he stood at the foot of a curved staircase in an old antebellum mansion, he riveted his eyes on Scarlett O'Hara. With his arm casually propped on the stair rail, he appeared like a fox hunting a spring hare. As she slowly walked up the stairs, Scarlet turned to a close friend and asked, "Catherine, who's that?" "Who?" Catherine responded. "That man looking at us and smiling. The nasty dog." "Dear, don't you know? That's Rhett Butler from Charlestown. He has the most terrible reputation."

In one of the most famous scenes in, *Gone with the Wind*, Rhett Butler never said a word. However, his position at the bottom of the staircase, as well as his relaxed and calculating manner, spoke volumes. His cool and confident air revealed a man who knew what he wanted and how to get it. He appeared to be enjoying his quarry from a distance, sizing up the hunt. Let us step back into the scene and examine every detail.

In that moment, both Rhett and Scarlet were oblivious to the buzz of activity below on the spacious main floor. Unbeknownst to them, they were about to enter an emerging world of romance and tension. They appeared to be the only two in the room. Catherine's position standing behind her friend helps the audience focus on Scarlett. Furthermore, the pair of southern belles were located at the mid-point of the staircase. The decision to continue to the second floor or return to meet, "that nasty dog," appeared firmly in Scarlett's court. Rhett Butler seemed willing to patiently wait for the dark-haired vixen to fall into his trap. In the world of theater and cinema, these actions are called blocking and body language, and they are vital to any story.

Blocking is simply the positions of the actors and actresses on the stage in relation to one another. Without this important element a scene can quickly dissolve into a chaotic mess. Stepping in front of a fellow actor, in the middle of an important line, confuses the audience. Excessive movement in the background can distract a crowd away from what should be the primary focus of the scene. Equally, the design of a stage and the placement of the props play a vital role.

Likewise, in the scene with Rhett and Scarlet, the use of body language is powerful. Again, Butler never utters a word. There is more expressed through the eyes than ever rolls off the thespian's tongue. A slight turn of the head tells the viewers how the villain might respond to an offer of kindness. A closeness in proximity between two actors can reveal intimacy, while standing far apart tends to expose tension. Furthermore, when a stage is filled with characters, blocking and body language help keep the focus on those who are telling the story.

On heaven's stage these vital elements are no less important, but with added dimensions. They involve how we interact with the Director and our relationships with whom we share life. Blocking in God's theater involves much more than simply knowing our place on the stage. Likewise, body language takes on an intrinsic value. These new dynamics are to become second nature, because in the kingdom of God, we are more than individuals who share a script, we are family.

When we enter God's theater we discover that relationships look differently than on the world's stage. It is not enough to simply know where to stand or how to fix our face. In fact, being a member of the cast of the Director brings certain expectations that run contrary to what we have always understood to be normal. There are new skills to develop and new avenues to consider. Old ways of doing things must come to a screeching halt. Our natural tendencies must give way to new spiritual practices. All this takes time as we must understand that we are now on higher ground.

First of all, this world teaches us the importance of self-promotion. The goal of each audition is to land the leading part. We naturally assume that our lines should be the most important in the production, even if we only have three. "Anything you can do I can do better," is the song softly sung in the wings.

William Shakespeare in, *Othello,* writes a tale of love and jealousy, of racial tension, and romantic intrigue. Iago, the sinister standard-bearer of Othello, becomes enraged at being overlooked for a promotion and plots the downfall of his master. When Iago attempts to drive Othello into a jealous rage by suggesting his wife, Desdemona, has been unfaithful, he tells his General, "oh beware, my lord, of jealousy. It is the green-eyed monster which doth mock the meat it feeds on." (3.3) At one point, Othello throws himself to ground in an epileptic fit.

The plot twists and turns as the antagonist, Iago, manipulates and manages a fine web of deceit with a number of characters in the story. Othello ends up killing his wife, Desdemona, but soon after discovers her innocence and the treachery of Iago. Rather than be taken back to Venice to be tried, Othello kills himself with a sword hidden in his cloak. Iago is ordered to be executed. Innocent people die and a good man is driven to madness through the "green-eyed monster of jealousy." Heaven's stage becomes a tragedy when self-centered agendas dominate.

James and John were called the sons of thunder. That's quite a title to be splashed across the marquee. Perhaps, it was a reference to their father Zebedee rather than his sons. Be that as it may, they were certainly two men on a mission. Images of their fiery spirits show up in the gospel narrative in a number of occasions. John tried to stop men who were casting out devils because they were not a part of the circle of disciples that Jesus had chosen. When the Samaritans rejected a visit from Jesus, James and John offered to burn them up with a few lightning strikes. A spirit of superiority had infected the apostolic band. What might have caused this glaring defect in these two disciples?

The apostles had just returned from a recent preaching tour. For the very first time they had witnessed the power of Christ through their own preaching and healing ministry. No doubt many had called on the name of Jesus for miracles. Imagine, to their surprise, when the crippled walked and the dumb sang praises to God. Through hands that once cleaned fish, the cleansing power of God moved. The apostles were being looked upon as men of God who could release people from their suffering. It is possible they began to look at themselves as special, and that is always the beginning of trouble. The idea that anyone would reject their Master inflamed them. The threat of others being involved in ministry challenged their hold on power. In the minds of the sons of thunder, heaven's stage needed to be kept small and firmly in their control. Jesus responded quickly.

The Master told his disciples to back away from the ministries of others. They had to realize that heaven's theater included a vast and diversified group of followers and not everyone was going to shuck the corn the same way. Jesus rebuked their harsh and critical spirits regarding the Samaritans. They needed to be reminded that the Director oversees his theater, and they were simply a part of what he was doing.

We soon discover that the Director rejects that approach as unacceptable. Our default mentality must be one of a servant. We must earnestly desire the advancement of our fellow actor. Our eyes must be constantly on the Director, not on others or ourselves. We must be constantly aware of our relationship first to the Lord and then to those with whom we share life. All eyes must be first directed to the One who sits in the highest chair.

Likewise, criticism of a fellow cast member is out of place. Its presence in our world is commonplace but on heaven's stage negativity sends a stench directly into the nose of the Director himself. Listening for the sake of condemnation also causes us to forget our own lines.

It is vital to understand how much the lights dim in heaven's theater when criticism enters the arena. It is a poison that spreads quickly and impacts deeply. The root of a critical spirit is found in the soil of our own insecurities. When we see our fellow actor as someone who could replace us on the stage of life, we begin to plot their downfall. The thought that someone else might outperform us reveals pride born of self-importance. A critical spirit backstage about the performance of others is a sure sign of self-doubt and envy. A desire to get the last word in and be seen as the one who always gets it right is the antithesis of the spirit of the Playwright. The attempt to climb new heights over the bodies of those we have stabbed only leads to our own demise. Such behavior quickly reveals itself to the entire cast. The Director frowns on a critical spirit as it spoils relationships and hurts fellow cast members. Narcissism is a curse within any life and especially on heaven's stage.

Chickens are fascinating creatures, but they can also be brutal. If one develops a wound, the others will pick at the chicken until it is dead. Salve must be applied quickly to rescue the hen from a foul end. The stage of life can resemble a chicken yard.

Likewise, the ocean is filled with danger. The fish that swim in the salt water and seaweed must play a treacherous game called eat or be eaten. Mankind plays the same game. We complicate things with a net and a hook when we feed on the downfall of others.

Seas and chicken yards offer up a daily reminder of life in its most treacherous form. Unfortunately, we can be much the same way and especially with those close to us. Criticism is a poison to any relationship and must be cast far from us. On heaven's stage all such behavior is out of place because it doesn't match the spirit of the Playwright. Our desire must be to build others up, not tear them down. Solomon wrote, "the tongue of the righteous is choice silver, and the lips of the righteous feed many."[146]

Servanthood is a key element in the arena of blocking and body language on heaven's stage. To cultivate an encouraging spirit toward others, we must shift our mindset away from personal recognition and onto a daily attitude of service to others. Looking around the stage to find the lowest seat is to be chosen over the spotlight. To discover the strengths and encourage the journey of our fellow actors is vastly more important than our part in the production. Our greatest legacy on heaven's stage is to bring out the best in others. However, we can't accomplish this by simply flipping a switch. Something more is required, and for the apostles, it began after the resurrection.

None of the disciples sought recognition after witnessing the glorified Christ. There is no evidence of their jockeying for position during his resurrection appearances. His private meetings with the disciples were marked by a quiet sense of shock and awe. They finally realized who they had been with for the last three years, and they were speechless.

When the Holy Spirit entered the upper room at Pentecost, all those present were transformed. Peter had his foot removed from his mouth. James and John had the thunder taken out of them, and Simon the Zealot pitched his "death to Rome" posters into a fire. Thomas never doubted again. All the disciples eventually died a martyr's death except for John.

In the presence of true greatness all other lights dim. To steal the credits when all acclaim belongs to Jesus is to willfully turn away from the reality of his glory. He is the hero of the story, and we are to be humble servants pointing out his majesty. The hidden lust for applause is foreign to the heart of a true servant. The lure of the limelight surely taints the Playwright's story. It is to create an idol of ourselves.

True servants do not place themselves in the role of defining what life looks like for others. We must be careful not to fit others into a mold of what we believe our fellow thespians ought to be doing. The desire to create our own image in the lives of others always ends in disaster. Within the heart of one person, servanthood means listening, but to another, it involves baking bread.

Martha and Mary were sisters, but they could not have been more different. Martha was always busy serving others while Mary focused her attention on people. So, when Jesus showed up for a meal, they both fell back on what came natural to them. Martha stirred the beans while Mary sat at the feet of Jesus. All would have been well, but Martha had a problem with her sister's lack of help in the kitchen. *No one gets fed until the bread gets baked,* she thought, *and Mary has left me to do all the work.* Martha could stand it no longer. Charging into the room she confronted Jesus. It is interesting that she did not confront her sister directly, but instead, she appealed to the Master. Apparently, she had tried before to mold Mary into a likeness of herself and failed. She was confident that Jesus would be on her side in the matter. We are no different. We are confident that the best image in others is our own.

Martha complained, "Lord, do you not care that my sister has left me to serve alone? Tell her then to help me,"[147] It is a red flag when we begin to dictate to the Director what the next scene should look like. Jesus patiently responded, ""Martha, Martha, you are anxious and troubled about many things, but one thing is necessary. Mary has chosen the good portion, which will not be taken away from her."[148] He was not criticizing Martha for serving. Jesus was gently rebuking her for attempting to control her sister's choice of ministry. Mary's quietness at Jesus's feet was just as significant as Martha's stew.

There is nothing more precious than a servant, but when that servant becomes bitter in ministry, the reward is lost, and the scene is spoiled. We all have a part to play in heaven's theater, and it is none of our business the roles others are given. To celebrate our differences is to be secure in the role we have been given. When we project our own viewpoint into the actions of others, we leave our own role and sit down in the Director's chair. It is also helpful to understand that our differences are intrinsic. They are placed there by the Creator.

In *Taming the Family Zoo*, Jim and Suzette Brawner have greatly aided us in understanding different personality types. They write, "About 400 years before Christ, Hippocrates, a Greek physician, divided the human race into four temperaments."[149] According to Jim and Suzette, these personality types include lions, otters, beavers, and golden retrievers. Lions are strong, assertive, and competitive. They are adventurous, goal-driven, and decisive. Otters are fun-loving. They avoid details, are optimistic, and enjoy change. Beavers are orderly, predictable, precise, and factual. They are persistent in whatever task they are given. Golden Retrievers are loyal, adaptable, and enjoy deep relationships.

Reflecting on the scene in Mary and Martha's home, it is easy to see their personalities in action. Martha, with her lion mentality, did not understand her sister's gentle golden retriever approach. Jesus, being a seamless balance of all four types, understood the situation perfectly.

Until we see that each actor is unique, and that God has a different path for all of us, we will continue to work toward an unnecessary equity on heaven's stage. It is a mark of maturity to celebrate the differences each actor and actress bring to the production. The life of Jesus, as it is seen in all our lives, looks differently. Jesus does not change our personalities. Instead, he uses our temperaments in the roles he wants us to play. He shines through us all in very unique ways.

The scene of Jesus walking down the shores of Galilee after his resurrection must have been beautiful. A gentle tide, washing over the round stones of the shoreline and the occasional seagull screaming overhead, created a surreal moment. Peter, his rough and tumble fisherman, was walking with him that morning and possibly pointing out good fishing spots. Peter was then told what kind of death he would suffer. Turning back, he saw John following them and asked, "Lord, what about this man?"

Peter's concern was born of love. He was no doubt concerned for the young man's future. If following Jesus would cost him a violent death what might this young and tender disciple have to endure. Perhaps, he felt it was his responsibility to protect the young man. Since Jesus was about to go back to heaven, his followers would need someone to watch out for them, he surmised. The response of Jesus was quick. "You follow me." He told Peter that it was none of his business where he placed his followers or what each had to endure.

The same God who cares for us certainly loves and cares for every actor and actress on his stage. When we attempt to rescue others from what God is doing in their lives, as cruel as it may seem at times, we are not following him. We unwittingly take the place of God by seeking to manipulate others or circumstances. We also blind ourselves from the opportunity to see what God is doing in their lives.

It is vital to engage with our fellow actors in meaningful ways in order to recognize God's promptings. This delicate art requires a perceptive eye and a listening ear. We cannot fully appreciate others and help them along their journey without seeing the work of Christ in their hearts. It is possible to have relationships wherein surface interactions are the standard. We must observe others not only for who they are, but also what they are becoming through Christ.

Dan and I had just finished a round of tennis. As we sat on the bench talking, he looked at me, and said, "I believe God is calling you to pastor a church." Before that moment, the thought had never entered my mind that my life would head in that direction. Looking back, it was certainly a moment that changed my life, and my friend was perceptive and bold enough to tell me what he was thinking. Dan did not have some revelation in the night that was mysterious and profound, he simply observed my life and what he perceived to be true. The ability to see God's work in the lives of others is not a fruit of the Spirit, it is the results of a keen eye. My friend saw something within me that I did not see myself. If we will but take the time, God may use us to encourage others on heaven's stage and point them to a new path.

The following is a story that my wife, Karen, tells… "Our youth group at church would go on visitation every Thursday night. We always paired up with a partner. Each of us would speak at every other door. We came to a house at a nearby neighborhood, and it was my turn to share the gospel. I was about 15 years old at the time. Although I was shy, the Lord always seemed to give me courage when sharing him. A young girl about my age, who had been working on homework, came to the door. I introduced myself and my partner. I shared with her the gospel and then asked her if she were to die, did she know where she would spend eternity. She replied that she didn't but would like to know. That night I had the opportunity of leading her to the Lord. The following Sunday she came to our church and was baptized. A few years later, when I was home from Bible college, I attended a Bible study that my former Sunday school teacher was giving on the book of John. To my surprise, the young lady I had led to the Lord was also there. She told me that she, too, was going to Bible college and studying missions. I never had contact with her after that, but it is my hope that she continued to serve the lord. We'll have a lot to share with one another when I meet her in heaven one day."

When we observe our fellow cast members' abilities and talents, we are seeing the potential that they possess. Normally, what a person loves to do, is likely the direction they need to pursue. I am suggesting that we simply point it out to them and give a word of admonition. Encouraging our fellow believers is a great privilege, and one we will look back on and relish. Likewise, we are changed by others as we choose to listen to their input. Discipleship is a two way street.

Paul told Timothy not to neglect the gift of God that had been given him by the laying on of hands. There was no power in the hands of those men to give Timothy any gift at all. His talents and abilities were from God alone. The laying on of hands was simply an affirmation prompted by observation of the gifts within Timothy. We know from Paul's writings that this young man was timid and shy. He needed encouragement to boldly walk out on heaven's stage. The remembrance of the men who acknowledged his ministry was to be a constant encouragement for the young man. Like the roar of a crowd as we sprint for the finish line, we feed off the energy of those who have gone before us and those who are pointing us toward the prize. God's work grows in the midst of community.

We communicate much more with our bodies than with our words. Our eyes shine when we are complimented, and our ears turn red when we are angry. Our faces turn pale at the sight of something or someone that terrifies us. Some hide it better than others, but we all tell the tale of our thoughts and emotions with full and undeniable body language. Body language is powerful, and those who learn to interpret it are far ahead on the stage of life. Pain, anxiety, joy, and concern are all easily visible in the faces of others. Words may deceive, but the eyes never lie.

It takes a perceptive spirit to read the manuscripts written on the hearts of others. If we are only concerned with our own little space on the stage of life, we will never experience the joy of seeing what the Playwright is doing in the lives of others. We will be like marbles in a bag simply scratching the surface of other marbles. God desires us to be a sack of grapes squashing and mashing ourselves into the lives of our fellow actors and actresses. It is sometimes messy to be involved in other people's lives, and it does not mean we will always be rewarded for the effort. However, the alternative is a cold walk across a dark and lonely stage.

Blocking practice is boring. To stand for hours while stage position assignments are given is akin to a slow death. The only reprieve in the agony is to be placed next to a friend. Regardless of the time it takes, the Director must have perfect symmetry among actors in each scene. There are a lot of moving parts, and we sometimes don't understand his directives. He constantly changes our blocking positions sending a steady stream of strange characters across our path. We may sometimes question a last minute substitution.

However, it is in the mixing of individuals that amazing things can occur. Those who we do not care for at first may become lifelong friends.

In the midst of loneliness, a bond may be kindled with another person that encourages us on our way. We ourselves can become different people through our interactions with others. In a mysterious way, the divine touch of the Playwright energizes the story through our relationships, giving our lives new dimensions.

The Castaway is a story about a man stranded on a deserted island after his plane crashed into the Pacific Ocean. Marooned for years, he became deranged and barbaric. However, his loneliness and distress were partially relieved when a volley ball became his only friend. At one point, he became angry at Wilson and kicked it into the surf. Realizing what he had done, he frantically went in search of his friend. His time, marooned on a deserted island, was a case study of what happens to a man when he is cut off from humanity. As much as other people irritate us, a year alone on an island makes us realize that we desperately need their company.

None of us were born in isolation, and it is equally true that none of us can survive well without our fellow man. The show simply cannot go on without others who sing and dance around us and with us. Without a band, the dance floor is useless. We were created by God to live in community with others, and any attempt to deny this truth by practice is an exercise in futility. Hermits come down from the hills to buy their yearly supplies with wild looks on their faces.

Life is not lived in a vacuum, and no man is an island. Success or failure in life is greatly dependent on our interactions with others. The key to healthy relationships is possessing a keen awareness of our position on life's stage at any given moment. We must learn to be perceptive in our interactions with our fellow stage members. As important as it is to know our lines, it is sometimes more important to read between the lines. Reading facial expressions and body language is an important skill. Being sensitive to others requires we live in the sphere of others. Pulling people into our bubble may be uncomfortable, but it is necessary for our growth.

Through blocking, he refines our lives and the lives of others. "Iron sharpens iron, and one man sharpens another."[150] Even those who oppose us can sharpen us in what we believe or give us direction for our lives. These changes may be invisible to us, and yet, clearly seen by heaven's audience. One key element of blocking and body language has yet to be discussed.

The movements on heaven's stage must have proper inspiration and power to be meaningful and lasting. Lesser motivations abound and can easily be identified. A steady frustration with others on the stage of life and burn-out are two such indicators. A dissatisfaction with life, especially in the midst of success, is another warning sign that our lives need more than applause. Jealousy is a red flag indicating low self-esteem. A life focused on our own abilities and strengths is soon exhausted. We obviously need a higher vision.

In a very real sense God has not called us to do anything. He has called us to himself. True spiritual blocking and body language is an organic reaction to a principle of life greater than our own. When Jesus said, "Come unto me," he was not referring to a single moment in our lives but a steady ongoing attitude of mind and heart. He was speaking to the weary. Jesus was offering a lifeline to the burdened soul.

Oswald Chambers once said, "Whenever marrings come to our lives it is because we have twisted off somewhere, we are not living in simple, full, child-like union with God, handing the keeping of our lives over to him and being carefully careless about everything saving our relationship to him; keep that right, and He will guard every avenue."[151]

Anything that lacks intense devotion to the Director will not carry the day. Apart from him our love will always fall short and quickly denigrate into self-reliance, self-promotion, self-advancement. A flower pulled up by its roots will soon wither. We will strive for a crown to be kept rather than one we can throw at his feet. The primary motivation must be the life of Jesus Christ within us.

All true service finds its source in Jesus Christ. He promises rest, and it is out of that reclined position that our service carries with it the touch of the Playwright. We naturally find the right position and the proper body language when we are guided by his gentle hand.

Solomon wrote, "there is a time to seek, and a time to lose; a time to keep, and a time to cast away; a time to tear, and a time to sow; a time to keep silence, and a time to speak; a time to love, and a time to hate; a time for war, and a time for peace."[152] True blocking and body language is knowing the perfect timing and acting accordingly. It is understanding the dynamic of each moment that we live and then listening to the Spirit's guidance. This can only be accomplished organically as our minds and hearts are focused on the Director. The Sermon on the Mount was not meant for us but for the life he would place in us at the point of redemption. Jesus was describing what life would look like as we rest in him. This alone is true blocking and body language on the stage of heaven.

CHAPTER 13

Cut, That's a Take

O n a movie set, unlike the theater, actors are given second chances. If a line is not delivered with the passion it deserves, or the timing is off, the Director simply says, "Cut." Everyone in the cast assumes their starting positions, and they take another run at the scene. Once the Director is happy he cries, "Cut, that's a take." It would be nice if life were like that, but it is not.

In the movie, *Napoleon Dynamite*, the character of Uncle Rico strikes a familiar chord. Bemoaning his lost opportunity of fame on the gridiron, he lives in the shadowlands of regret. If only the coach had put him in, he would have thrown the winning pass and had a different life. Glory denied, Uncle Rico lives in a camper in the middle of nowhere, throwing a football to the ghost of his lost opportunity of fame. He refuses to move on, and instead, lives in the yesteryear of what could have been.

Throughout life we are hit squarely between the eyes with this unrelenting truth; there are no retakes. "Better march out on that stage and give it your all," we're admonished. "You only get one shot to get it right." "When the moments pass, they are gone forever." "What has been done, has been done," we surmise. There is nothing to be done but wait for life's final curtain. It would be nice to have a time machine, to send us back to the scenes of our greatest crimes, our deepest regrets. If Uncle

Rico could only go backward in time and throw that winning pass. A life do-over would be appreciated.

However, even if time travel were possible, and Uncle Rico tried, our fellow actors and actresses have moved on. Our displeasure with our performance means nothing to them now, if it ever did. It is also impossible to reconstruct the moment as it was originally shot, and so, we are left to imagine the path denied. Failed opportunities rain on our parade, causing us to lose focus in the here and now. The seeds of yesterday's failures produce ugly weeds in a garden that should be filled with the flowers of today. The unwelcomed hound of disappointment follows us to our graves.

At other times, we romanticize our past. We create scenes that never happened, filled with glory that was nonexistent at the first take. Our breath-stealing mental reenactments were rarely true. The knight in shining armor was really a peasant on a mule, and the belle of the ball was a wall flower. Our teen romance was a mess of youthful foolishness, but we somehow remember it as a Romeo and Juliet love affair. We imagine our picture hanging prominently on the wall of our high school, but few even remember our name. We simply weren't as grand as our memories tell us. A reconstructive history suits us.

Regardless of which fantasy we indulge; it is one of God's specialties to bring his purposes out of our messy past and point us toward the true glory that is to be our future. You see, God has always been busy at work in our lives, and he continues to this day. He uses the scraps of our past and our present path to weave his eternal plan into our lives. We may view ourselves as over-the-hill or beyond repair, but God is still patiently at work in us. Concerning our past, nothing goes to waste in the theater of the Director's gracious overview. God uses our wasted opportunities and failures as his opportunity to mold us.

On the stage of heaven, the Playwright is always forward focused. He doesn't waste time replaying our failures in his mind and wishing he had picked someone else. And so, it is vital that we leave yesterday's performances behind. The Bible says that the gifts and callings of God are without regret.[153] He knew us long before he chose us for his story, and no failure on our part could ever cause him to wring his hands and look for a replacement. We may sit backstage filled with remorse over a missed line or movement, but the Playwright is somehow pleased with how the show is progressing. Sitting despondent in the wings, we hear our name called, and it's showtime again.

Furthermore, he knows what he is after and is relentless in his pursuit. He will not rest until he sees the reflection of His Son in us. "My little children, for whom I am again in the anguish of childbirth until Christ is formed in you!"[154] In six days God created all that we enjoy around us, and yet, his work within us takes longer, and he remains patient. Just when we think the show is over, he cries, "Take two." Even a colossal collapse doesn't slow the Director down, which is exactly what a big fisherman discovered long ago.

Peter had made enough stage blunders to earn himself a trip back to acting school. On the Mount of Transfiguration, he spoke when he should have been quiet. He got into an argument with the other disciples concerning who was the greatest, and when children were brought to Jesus, he tried to send them away. At one point Jesus told Peter to get behind him, even calling him Satan. That's a low, low moment!

However, the crowning disaster that could have defined Peter for the rest of his life began in the Garden of Gethsemane and ended at a nearby fire. Peter swung a sword at a Roman soldier, ran into the darkness to avoid capture, and then denied Jesus three times to a harmless girl while warming his hands over the enemy's fire. Hands down, it was a total collapse.

The nosebleed section should have been Peter's lot. He should have been handed a pair of binoculars and told to sit down and be quiet. Nevertheless, on the day of Pentecost, there he was, full-throated and preaching like there was no tomorrow or, more importantly, no yesterday. If he would have allowed his heart to sideline him, he would have missed delivering one of the greatest sermons ever heard. That day thousands were called onto heaven's stage, and the rugged fisherman was in the mix.

Years later, Peter was rebuked by Paul because he hadn't read the script carefully enough concerning God's work to bring the Gentiles into the fold. "But when Cephas came to Antioch, I opposed him to his face, because he stood condemned. For before certain men came from James, he was eating with the Gentiles; but when they came he drew back and separated himself, fearing the circumcision party."[155] Peter chose religious respectability instead of love. The fear of man had snared him. After years of serving Christ, Peter was still producing some bad scenes.

However, unwilling to be defined by his miscues, Peter went on to a life of service and ministry. He wrote two letters in the New Testament and was instrumental in strengthening first century churches. His last performance was on a cross in Rome, insisting he be crucified upside down because he felt unworthy to die like his Master. At the end of his life Peter wrote this, "But even if you should suffer for righteousness' sake, you will be blessed. Have no fear of them, nor be troubled."[156] There was no mention of his past sins throughout any of his writings.

It is difficult to look back and see the mess we've made of things. Allowing our minds to become fixated on our failures, the lights suddenly go dim, and it appears there will be no sequel. Roads become dead ends with nowhere to turn off. Pushed into a lonely side street behind the theater, we begin to walk away only to hear the Director crack the door and tell us to hurry back because we are in the next scene.

Looking back at the most disastrous moments of our lives, he was there with the next scene in hand. It takes courage to step back out on that stage. You are not the first to fail him, neither will you be the last. If we only understood how much he loves us, we would think less of our own messiness and more of how he has completely cleaned us up. We must face our fears with a firm confidence in the Lord's power to restore.

All too often, though, our fears slow our progress in life. When the bitter taste of failure fills our palate, it is difficult to taste anything else. Our taste buds are never the same, or so we think. We spilled the chili, and so, we shall never carry chili again. We got turned down for a date, so we remain single. The interview did not go well, and so, we are convinced we are not good at answering questions under pressure. The list could go on and on.

There is always an excuse to keep us in the safe place. "The sluggard says, "There is a lion in the road! There is a lion in the streets!"[157] The twin lions of past failure and future fear cripples our souls and paralyzes our need to grow into new roles in God's production. Courage, though, is not born in the absence of fear but in its presence. When doubt and misgivings surround us, we must make a choice. Do I believe that God can still use my life, or will I embrace the lie that I am finished on heaven's stage? More importantly, am I convinced of the forgiveness of God? Our decisions, in the crucibles of catastrophe, determines our future roles as nothing else does.

L. Frank Baum, the author of *The Wonderful Wizard of Oz,* suffered as a child from frequent nightmares. His reoccurring dream about a scarecrow chasing him across a hayfield left him terrified. Moments from being gripped with his "ragged hay fingers," the scarecrow would suddenly fall apart before his eyes. Perhaps, Baum wrote the scarecrow into the story as a means of facing and conquering the fear he had of them as a child. Whatever his reason, the experience helped create a fascinating character in his book. The struggle to overcome fear in itself can be a catalyst for new areas of creativity and growth in our lives. Jesus taught, "Therefore, do not be anxious about tomorrow, for tomorrow will be anxious for itself. Sufficient for the day is its own trouble."[158] It all begins by our confidence in the Director.

Now, there are things that are not our cup of tea. We should leave those "things" alone. If you can't carry a note, don't carry your voice up on a stage in front of people. However, if we allow the fear of launching out into new adventures to whither on the vine, we will look back with regret. If we succumb to our anxieties, we will sit in dark rooms sipping weak tea and eating stale crackers. We will shun the stage on which the Director is calling us. Courage is found by listening to the voice of the One who says, "Be strong and courageous. Do not fear or be in dread of them, for it is the LORD your God who goes with you. He will not leave you or forsake you."[159]

It is also the practice of God to keep silent regarding our part in the overall production. He does not lay out the entire script before us. The scenes of our lives are delivered on a daily basis to our dressing room. Abraham was told to leave Ur of the Chaldeans, and he went out, "not knowing where he was going."[160] David was tending sheep when he was interrupted by the prophet Samuel. Paul was on a search and destroy mission to Damascus when he was stopped dead in his tracks. None of these men knew what to expect beyond the initial call. They just knew who was calling them.

The Playwright's habit of giving daily instructions only keeps us off-balance. Being in the constant clutches of confusion regarding tomorrow's scenes produces what Oswald Chamber called the graciousness of uncertainty. "All through the Bible the realm of the uncertain is the realm of joy and delight; the certainty of belief brings distress. Certainty of God means uncertainty in life, while certainty in belief makes us uncertain of God. Certainty is the mark of the common sense life; gracious uncertainty is the mark of the spiritual life, and they must both go together. Mathematics is the rule of reason and common sense, but faith and hope are the rule of the spiritual."[161] Jesus said succinctly, "But seek first the kingdom of God and his righteousness, and all these things will be added to you."[162] By keeping us focused on each day's business, we are forced to keep our eyes on the Director. In doing so, we accomplish God's will.

The Tyranny of the Urgent, written by Charles E. Hummel, is a small, punchy pamphlet. In it he provides profound truths anchored in the life and ministry of Jesus. "In his earthly life, Jesus chose to limit himself by time and space. The geographical scope of his life's work was quite small. Jesus never traveled to any land outside of Israel except for a few trips into lands north of Galilee. Rather than healing everyone he encountered, he only touched those who had faith. In his own hometown of Nazareth, he could do no mighty works because they did not believe. His life was never feverish; he had time for people. He could spend hours talking to one person, such as the Samaritan woman at the well. His life showed a wonderful balance, a sense of timing."[163] Jesus was never gripped by the anxiety of completing a lifetime of activity in one day. He simply did what the Father told him to do each day. Manna was given to the Jews in the wilderness on a daily basis. In the same way, the Director knows that life is best served in daily portions.

God is in no hurry. He knows what he is about, and he is willing to hold onto our lines until he is ready for our part to be played. Times of inactivity drive us mad. We stare at the curtain longing for it to rise and it collects dust. Occupying mainstage is our constant obsession. Perhaps that is why, "he makes us lie down in green pastures, beside the still waters."[164] Notice he has to *make* us lie down. We itch for the busy life.

In the interim, our temptation is to exit through a side door and wander down rabbit holes to occupy our time with frivolous pursuits. Idleness drives us into a frenzy the likes of a Mad Hatter at six o'clock tea. There sits the sleepy Dormouse, the March Hare, and Alice, unable to answer the Hatter's nonsensical riddle, "why is the raven like a writing desk?" The riddle cannot be solved, but what does that matter, at least we are sipping tea. We much prefer doing something rather than nothing. God, in contrast, patiently waits for our growth, and he knows when our next scene will be shot. He is comfortable with our dormancy while he works his life into us. The mighty oak spends most of the year solidifying its sap into fibrous wood.

The script of our life is written in heaven, but the Playwright also allows us to act it out using our own emerging talents and abilities. Enter the joy of the improv as expressed through our ever-changing growth in character and spiritual maturity. The Bible itself was written by men as they were moved by the Holy Spirit.[165] The personalities of those writers were factored in, and yet, in the end, the ink that flowed was directly from the Author. It all came together perfectly, and we have the word of God as the result. Our part in his story is a mix of divine directives and our personalities on full display. Heaven's theater is the perfect fusion of divine structure and human clutter. Perfection born out of chaos is his technique. A theater filled with robotic actors and actresses is not the vision of the Playwright. He is patching together the quilt of his story one stitch at a time. He has written a rigidly fluid play.

Consider the tender, overriding, matchless hand of the Playwright. Each day begins with the sun being called out of its slumber, and every sunset is his decision that the day is done. The hummingbird that flies by our shoulder was sent by him and each waking moment is by his design and delight. Our next breath is in his hand, and the rhythm of our heartbeat matches his cadence. In the night hours he is busy behind the scenes perfecting the set by moving all the props into place for the next day. The Director never sleeps. The Psalmist cried out, "My hope comes from the Lord who made heaven and earth. He will not let your foot be moved; he who keeps you will not slumber. Behold, he who keeps Israel will neither slumber nor sleep."[166] He is always in the wings directing traffic as he turns our lives into a thing of beauty. From God's perspective three things come quickly into view.

First, our lives are valuable beyond comprehension simply because he created us. Regardless of our limitations, we were formed and fashioned by an all-knowing God. This truth, though, cannot be fully appreciated it until is embraced by faith. A diamond cannot be properly appraised by a chicken scratching in the dirt. She much prefers the worms she finds in the soil. We must lift our eyes above the common fray to see our true value. If origin determines worth and value, then we are all in a good place.

Moreover, our personal worth on heaven's stage is bound up in the simple truth that the Scriptwriter has placed us on the stage of life for a particular purpose. "When once you realize the Divine purpose behind your life you will never say again, 'I am so weak'; you will know you are, but you will be strong in His strength. The only strength we have is the strength of God which comes to us from the vision of God and his power."[167] God has specific designs for our lives.

Secondly, for the believer in Christ, the significance of our years spent on earth are not over with the closing of our casket. My father-in-law's name was John T. Nutt. At his funeral, the preacher happily exclaimed that Nutt had been shelled out and was now in heaven. The husk of his life down here had been removed, exposing a richer life up there. All the deep desires of his life were now being fulfilled by the One who does all things well.

The Beatitudes teach a future fulfillment for those who hunger and thirst now. Jesus told his disciples, "Blessed are you who are poor, for yours is the kingdom of God. Blessed are you who are hungry now, for you should be satisfied. Blessed are you who weep now, for you shall laugh."[168]

Randy Alcorn, in his book simply titled, *Heaven,* writes concerning the possibility that the unfinished business of this life will be carried on and completed in heaven. "I believe the New Earth will offer us possibilities we wished for but never had. God's original plan was that human beings would live happy and fulfilling lives on earth. If our current lives are our only chance of that, God's plan has been thwarted. Consider the injustice that many honest people never got to live fulfilling lives while some dishonest and unfaithful people seem to fare much better."[169]

The moments we regret, as well as the unfinished business of our lives, is not left undone from God's standpoint. All the loose ends will be tied up perfectly after we have exited stage left. In heaven, God heals all wounds and helps us to make sense of the messiness of life. Like my father-in-law, the hard shell of our life down here is discarded. Relationships that struggled in this life will be healed in the next. Our outward failings and disappointments are gone, revealing the true beauty of God's work in our lives.

Heaven is not a place of regret but of unbounded joy. We will look back and be amazed at what God did through our lives. Each day will make sense. Our story will be reviewed as one grand finale plays out before our eyes. Encore after encore will shake the courts of the New Jerusalem. Dorothy was right to sing, "Somewhere over the rainbow way up high. There's a land that I heard of once in a lullaby. Somewhere over the rainbow skies are blue, and the dreams that you dare to dream, really do come true."[170]

Lastly, our lives contain a thread which travels well into the future, having been impacted by those who came before us. Aaron Smith was one of the few brave men who crossed the Delaware River with General Washington on December 25th, 1776. Aaron Smith was my grandfather, seven generations back, who against incredible hardships, fought alongside the likes of Alexander Hamilton and Henry Knox in defeating the German Hessians at Trenton, New Jersey. It was a battle that changed the tide of the Revolutionary War giving us the freedom we enjoy today. I carry his legacy.

I can still see my Grandma Smith's thick, worn Bible sitting on her nightstand. Her faith in Christ seemed real to me as a little boy. Her life was a testament to her faith in God. There were other events that had an impact on my early life. Sunday mornings in our household included listening to Tennessee Ernie Ford belt out the old hymns through an old phonograph player. My father sitting by an old dusty turntable listening to Ford's deep voice sing, *Great is thy Faithfulness,* is a memory I shall never forget. While returning home from school one day I saw my mother hanging dangerously out of a second-floor window so she could clean it properly. She loved her family enough to provide a clean home. These were small things that grew in time to become meaningful recollections for me.

In the countryside of Middlefield, New York, Michael Galer farmed the land. As his wife lay sick at home, my great grandfather Galer collapsed on the back of a hay wagon and died. His wife, Sarah Irish Galer, died the next day. At the age of 76, he still worked hard to provide for his wife and family. Faithful until the end, they both displayed an unending love and devotion for each other. His work ethic is an inspiration to me. Her broken heart at his death hastened her own demise. Buried together, their heritage is a meaningful part of my journey.

In the same way, our tale will be retold by the generations following us, hopefully to their blessing and our honor. God uses our story in the lives of others in ways we cannot imagine. Consider a story from the Old Testament.

The prophet Elijah performed 16 miracles during his life. Just before the chariot of fire took him to glory he asked his successor, Elisha, to make a final request. The young man requested a double portion of the blessing that Elijah had been given during his ministry which amounted to 32 miracles. When Elisha died years later he had only performed thirty-one miracles. Elisha was one short but even after death God was not done writing his story. "And as a man was being buried, behold, a marauding band was seen and the man was thrown into the grave of Elisha, and as soon as the man touched the bones of Elisha, he revived and stood on his feet."[171] Behold, the 32nd miracle. Elisha's skeleton was still a source of life.

Likewise, as our bones turn to dust, those who knew us well will still be telling our stories, and in some cases, modeling their lives after us. Our dry bones will continue to impact our families and friends in powerful ways that even they do not understand. We are not only buried in the clay of earth but in the hearts of those who have known us. The long chapters which are written in the hearts of our loved ones will tell a greater story than the words inscribed on our tombstone. In that day, the Director will cry out…, "Cut, that's a take."

CHAPTER 14

Encore

Death is not the end. Our lives in this world are but the prologue of a narrative that will never have an epilogue. In many ways, our inevitable demise in the clutches of death is only the beginning place of new and exciting adventures in heaven. The wind section in the orchestra will not pack up its instruments when we breath our last, and the stage lights will not dim as our eyelids close. In fact, our eyes will open to sights unimaginable and require descriptive language we do not presently possess. The celestial bagpipes will ring loud and clear welcoming us to grassy shores. On that eternal stage our performance will never hit a closing note. The story God is writing during our time on earth continues even after the purple velvet of a casket lid has pressed against our face and flowery eulogies have been spoken. There *is* an encore.

Once in heaven, the flow of an endless tide will wash back over our past life on this earth, and all will appear as if we have been in heaven from the start. All suffering and heartache will be healed and be seen as something glorious. At the point of our deepest sorrow, we will finally see the hand of God and be filled with joy. C.S. Lewis writes, "They say of some temporal suffering, 'No future bliss can make up for it,' not knowing that Heaven, once obtained, will work backwards and turn even that agony into a glory."[172]

In the same way that the opening scene of a play contains the seed plot for the entire story, our lives will come to full and glorious fruition in heaven. With expanded storylines, God's amazing tale will flourish. The bud that contains limitless potential will explode into fullness when we join the Playwright in heaven. Our role in that celestial theater will discover its true destiny.

American revivalist preacher, Jonathan Edwards, of the 17th century, wrote, "How happy is that love in which there is an eternal progress in all things; wherein new beauties are continually discovered, and more and more loveliness, and in which we shall forever increase in beauty ourselves; where we shall be made capable of finding out and giving, and shall receive, more and more enduring expressions of love forever: our union will become close, and communication more intimate."[173] Heaven will build on the foundation of our journey in this life as the best is yet to come.

Our future on that golden shore is unshakeable. Joining with the saints of all the ages, a celebration will occur the likes we can't begin to describe. The writer of Hebrews was convinced, "But you have come to Mount Zion and to the city of the living God, the heavenly Jerusalem, and to innumerable angels in festal gathering, and to the assembly of the firstborn who are enrolled in heaven, and to God, the judge of all, and to the spirits of the righteous made perfect, and to Jesus, the mediator of a new covenant, and to the sprinkled blood that speaks a better word than the blood of Abel."[174] It will be a cast party like no other.

However, our reunion with friends and loved ones is only the beginning. The sights and sounds of that city will pale in comparison to meeting the great Director. Moses walked down from Mount Sinai's cloud-covered peak with glory on his face. Isaiah was overcome in the temple at Jerusalem when he beheld the majesty of the Lord. Daniel fainted when he witnessed the Angel of the Lord by the Tigris River. Paul the Apostle became as a dead man when he met the risen Christ on the road to Damascus. In our glorified body we will stand before him.

Imagine the excitement of God as he awaits our first day in the Heavenly City. Paul states, "But, as it is written, 'What no eye has seen, nor ear heard, nor the heart of man imagined, what God has prepared for those who love him'"[175] Heaven's first day will be thrilling as we witness firsthand what he has prepared for us. It will require the rolling tides of eternity to discover the ever-unfolding treasures that are awaiting us.

The stories that we love most in the theater are those where justice is served, and the weakest soul gains the greatest reward. Those who offer the thirsty a cup of water will be rewarded. Caring for the incarcerated will have its own trophy. The meek shall inherent the earth in a way that fulfills all of God's promises to Israel and the church. Every prophecy will be fulfilled.

Charles Spurgeon admonishes us, "Christian, meditate much on heaven, it will help thee to press on, and to forget the toil of the way. This veil of tears is but the pathway to the better country: this world of woe is but the stepping-stone to a world of bliss. And, after death, what cometh? What wonder-world will open upon our astonished sight?"[176]

As the flowers in a garden turn and lean toward the sun for warmth, we look forward to that day when Jesus will appear. Hearts that grieve will explode with joy. Some warn us not to be too heavenly minded. If our minds are too occupied above, they remind us with a measured grin, we will be of no earthly good. Nothing could be further from the truth. The soul who has its focus on heaven does the earth the greatest good. "If then you have been raised with Christ, seek the things that are above, where Christ is, seated at the right hand of God. Set your minds on things that are above, not on things that are on earth."[177] We enhance the world we live in by proclaiming our true citizenship in heaven.

However, all this anticipation of heaven comes with a solemn warning. It is a sad, but abiding truth, that most will not enter that blessed city. The glories of heaven and eternal life are reserved only for those who have believed on Jesus Christ as Savior. The offer is free and full for all to come, but it is reliant on our decision to believe in the Redeemer. "The Spirit and the Bride say, 'Come.' And let the one who hears say, 'Come.' And let the one who is thirsty come; let the one who desires take the water of life without price."[178] The lives of Cain and Abel illustrate perfectly the two paths that are open to all humanity.

Abel raised sheep while his brother Cain grew crops. They, together with their sisters, formed the first family. All we know of Abel comes from an account in the book of Genesis wherein he brought an acceptable offering to God. The blood of an innocent animal was offered to God for a sacrifice. The basis of this bloody gift was obedience which flowed from

Abel's faith in what God had told him to do. As a result, the Lord received his offering. That's all we know about Abel other than the fact that he was murdered by his brother. However, the story doesn't end there.

Cain also brought a gift. His, though, was an offering of his own choosing. He brought the fruit of the ground. The bloodless offering was not what God required, and it was promptly rejected. Filled with anger and jealousy, Cain killed Abel. These two offerings speak to the whole matter of salvation. Abel believed God and brought the blood sacrifice and was accepted. Cain ignored God's command, and his offering was rejected. Why is this significant?

It requires a blood offering to cover sin. The purpose for the death of Jesus was to remove our sin completely and free us from its penalty and bondage. His blood did more than just cover our sins, it put them away forever. "As far as the east is from the west, so far does he remove our transgressions from us."[179]

However, we must believe in order to receive eternal life. The choice is ours. We can either bring the righteous offering that God requires, like Abel, or attempt to come to God on our own terms, through our own efforts, like Cain. He loves and respects us too much to ever force himself upon us. He will not violate our free well, even in the rejection of his Son.

C.S. Lewis writes, "There are only two kinds of people in the end: those who say to God, 'Thy will be done,' and those to whom God says, in the end, '*Thy* will be done.' All that are in Hell, choose it. Without that self-choice there could be no Hell."[180] God desires all men to be saved. "This is good, and it is pleasing in the sight of God our Savior, who desires all people to be saved and to come to the knowledge of the truth."[181] His hope is to write an endless series of chronicles revealing his handiwork in us. Come to him today. "For he says, 'In a favorable time I listened to you, and in a day of salvation I have helped you.' Behold, now is the favorable time; behold, now is the day of salvation."[182] The moments of our life will soon be swept away like a summer cloud. It is those who choose the Good Shepherd that will find rest for their souls.

One day I will walk into our town library and find that the story of my life is complete. I will take time to read what God has done and be glad. Entering heaven, I will finally meet the Great Storyteller and rejoice to see that his pen never runs dry. The weariness that writers experience is unknown to him who holds heaven's quill. The same ink that penned our stories will continue to chronicle his glory. The credits will never stop rolling on our life's narrative as he rightfully receives all the credit. *The End* will never appear across the silver screen of our lives. Heaven's stage awaits those who choose to dance life's greatest jig..

"Someday you will read in the papers that I am dead. Don't believe a word of it! At that moment I shall be more alive than I am now; I shall have gone up higher, that is all, out of this old clay tenement into a house that is immortal—a body that death cannot touch, that sin cannot taint; a body fashioned like unto His glorious body."

DWIGHT L. MOODY

Endnotes

1   Psalm 139:13,15-16
2   Psalm 139:1-4
3   Psalm 139: 8 KJV
4   Psalm 139:14b
5   1 Peter 1:12
6   Luke 18:10
7   Warner, Melanie Torres, Amber, *Angels Among Us* (Defining Moments Press), 19.
8   Daniel 10
9   Numbers 22
10 Acts 12:7
11 Hebrew 13:2
12 Tozer, A.W., *Pursuit of God* (Moody Publishers), 60,61.
13 Hebrews 12:1
14 Acts 17:26-28
15 Romans 11:29 KJV
16 Brand, Paul, Yancy, Philip, *Fearfully and Wonderfully Made* (Intervarsity Press), 38.
17 1 Corinthians 12:12
18 Brand, Paul Yancy, Philip, *Fearfully and Wonderfully Made* (Intervarsity Press), 39.
19 Henley, William Ernest, *"Invictus" from Poems* (London: Macmillan and Co., 1920), 83-84.
20 2 Corinthians 10:12
21 Ecclesiastes 1:3
22 Ecclesiastes 1:2
23 Gibbon, Edward, *The Decline and Fall of the Roman Empire Volume 1* (East India Publishing Company), 103.

24   Chambers, Oswald, *The Complete Works of Oswald Chambers* (Discovery House), 49.
25   Livgren, Kerry, *Dust in the Wind* (1977)
26   Ecclesiastes 1:3,4,9
27   Chambers, Oswald, *The Complete Works of Oswald Chambers* (Discovery House), 1195.
28   Matthew 6:33
29   Swindoll, Charles, *Abraham* (Tyndale House Publishers, Inc), 271.
30   Ecclesiastes 3:11
31   Interestingliterature.com (2020-5)
32   Plato, socratic-method.com (September 27, 2023)
33   Ephesians 4:18
34   John 1:4,5
35   Luke 9:23
36   Luke 12:32
37   Purdum, Todd S, *Something Wonderful* (Henry Holt and Company), 16.
38   Ecclesiastes 1:8
39   John 1:47,48
40   Grant, Ulysses S., *The Complete Personal Memoirs of General Ulysses S Grant* (Charles L. Webster and Company), 145.
41   Ibid. 145.
42   Ibid. 145.
43   Herman, Arthur, *The Viking Heart; How Scandinavia Conquered the World* (Houghton Mifflin Harcourt), 13.
44   1 Corinthians 1:27
45   McCullough, David, *1776* (Simon Schuster Paperbacks), 49.
46   Esther 4:14
47   Esther 4:16
48   Chambers, Oswald, *The Complete Works of Oswald Chambers* (Discovery House), 906.
49   Jeremiah 26:11
50   Daniel 12:3
51   Martin, Rachel L., americanhistory.si.edu
52   Psalm 139:15
53   Ecclesiastes 7:14
54   Isaiah 55:8
55   Genesis 1:1
56   Ecclesiastes 7:13
57   Burns, Robert, *To the Mouse* (poetryfoundation.org>poems), 1785.
58   Romans 11:29
59   Lewis, C.S., *Surprised by Joy* (A Harvest Book-Harcourt Inc), 229.

60   Ibid. 229
61   Ibid. 228.
62   Ibid. 226.
63   Ibid. 211.
64   Matthew 5:45
65   Nagler, A.M., *A Source Book in Theatrical History* (Dover Publication), 493.
66   Ecclesiastes 5:2
67   Daniel 4:29-30
68   Daniel 4:34-35
69   Acts 9:4
70   1 John 4:19
71   Tozer, A.W., *Pursuit of God* (Moody Publishers Chicago), 9.
72   Romans 3:11-12
73   Romans 3:19
74   Lewis, C.S., *The Weight of Glory* (USA: The Macmillan Co), 10.
75   Keneally, Thomas Michael, *Schindler's List* (goodquotes.com)
76   Tozer, A.W., *I Talk Back to the Devil; Essays in Spiritual Perfection* (1990)
77   Chambers, Oswald, *The Complete Works of Oswald Chambers* (Discovery House), 994.
78   McCullough, David, *The Path Between Two Seas* (Simon Schuster Paperbacks), 412.
79   Romans 8:28
80   2 Corinthians 1:3,4
81   Acts 22:20
82   Letslearnslang.com 14
83   Revelation 21:21
84   Davis, Patricia K., *A Midnight Carol* (St. Martin's Paperbacks), 2.
85   Chambers, Oswald, *The Complete Works of Oswald Chambers* (Discovery House), 1195.
86   Philippians 2:6-7
87   2 Corinthians 5:21
88   Genesis 2:7
89   2 Corinthians 4:7
90   Ecclesiastes 2:15
91   Habakkuk 1:4
92   Lowell, James Russell, *The Present Crisis* (poets.org)
93   Acts 17:6a
94   Twain, Mark, *The Adventures of Tom Sawyer* (Printed by Amazon), 191.
95   www.newyorker.com August 3.
96   Ibid.
97   Jeremiah 1:8

[98]   Miner, Henry Clay, www.hmdb.org

[99]   Pearce, Joseph Chilton, www.socraticmethod.com

[100] Proverbs 26:13

[101] Swindell, Charles, *Dropping Your Guard* (Word Books), XXI

[102] quoteinvestigator.com 2014.

[103] *The Masks That We Wear*, Psychology Today, October 20, 2015

[104] Genesis 10:8-9

[105] John 12:31

[106] Luke 10:18

[107] Isaiah 14:16

[108] Revelation 20:10

[109] Luke 10:19

[110] 1Peter 5:8

[111] 1John 4:4

[112] Stagebeauty.net (copyright 2007)

[113] Matthew 4:19

[114] Grann, David, *The Wager-A Tale of Shipwreck, Mutiny and Murder* (Doubleday Publishers), 158.

[115] Ibid.

[116] Gaylor, M.J., *The Seventh Trail- Journey to the Well of Chayah* (Xulon Press), 55.

[117] Gaylor, M.J., *Man's Search for Cabadgery* (Xulon Press), 58.

[118] 2 Corinthians 4:4

[119] Hebrews 2:7

[120] Rudd, Jay, *Mythlore 53, Fantasies of the Middle Earth* (mythsoc.org)

[121] Lewis, C.S., The Lion, the Witch, and the Wardrobe (Harper Trophy), 138,139.

[122] Rudd, Jay, *Mythlore 53, Fantasies of the Middle Earth* (mythsoc.org)

[123] Lewis, C.S., *The Lion, the Witch, and the Wardrobe* (Harper Trophy), 138,139.

[124] Rudd, Jay, *Mythlore 53, Fantasies of the Middle Earth* (mythsoc.org)

[125] 1Peter 1:18-20

[126] Genesis 22:7b

[127] Romans 8:37 KJV

[128] Joshua 10:24

[129] Joshua 10:25

[130] Dickens, Charles, *David Copperfield* (Bradbury & Evan), 1.

[131] Matthew 7:13-14

[132] McCarthy, Mary, goodquotes.com.

[133] Romans 6:14

[134] Ecclesiastes 3:4

[135] atimetolaugh.org

[136] mayoclinic.org

[137] Ibid.

138 Proverbs 17:22
139 Job 8:21
140 1 Samuel 18:7
141 Mark 6:31
142 Havner, Vance, *Pepper 'n Salt* (Fleming H. Revell Company).
143 Psalm 2:4
144 Isaiah 53:3
145 2 Samuel 9:1
146 Proverbs 10:20-21
147 Luke 10:40
148 Luke 10:41-42
149 Brawner, Jim and Suzette, *Taming the Family Zoo* (NavPress Publishing Company), 30.
150 Proverbs 27:17
151 Chambers, Oswald, *The Complete Works of Oswald Chambers* (Discovery House), 579.
152 Ecclesiastes 3:7-8
153 Romans 11:29
154 Galatians 4:19
155 Galatians 2:11-12
156 1 Peter 3:14
157 Proverbs 26:13
158 Matthew 6:34
159 Deuteronomy 31:6
160 Hebrews 11:8
161 Chambers, Oswald, *The Complete Works of Oswald Chambers* (Discovery House), 688.
162 Matthew 6:33
163 Hummel, Charles E., *The Tyranny of the Urgent* (Inter-Varsity Press), 8.
164 Psalm 23:2
165 2 Peter 1:21
166 Psalm 121:4
167 Chambers, Oswald, *The Complete Works of Oswald Chambers* (Discovery House), 1392.
168 Matthew 5
169 Alcorn, Randy, *Heaven* (Tyndale House Publishers, Inc), 416.
170 Arlen, Harold, Harburg, Yip, *The Wizard of Oz*
171 2 Kings 13:21
172 Lewis, C.S., *The Great Divorce* (Simon & Schuster), 67.
173 Alcorn, Randy, *Heaven* (Tyndale House Publishers, Inc), 331.
174 Hebrews 12:22-24

[175] 1Corinthians 2:9

[176] Ibid. 322.

[177] Colossians 3:1,2

[178] Revelation 22:17

[179] Psalm 103:12

[180] Lewis, C.S., *The Great Divorce* (Simon & Schuster), 72.

[181] 1 Timothy 2:3,4

[182] 2 Corinthians 6:2

Bisbeesworld.org

Printed in the United States
by Baker & Taylor Publisher Services